EVERYONE BELONGS

HUMAN HORIZONS SERIES

EVERYONE BELONGS

Mainstream Education for Children with Severe Learning Difficulties

Kenn Jupp

A CONDOR BOOK
SOUVENIR PRESS (E & A) LTD

First published 1992 by Souvenir Press
(Educational & Academic) Ltd,
43 Great Russell Street, London WC1B 3PA
and simultaneously in Canada

ISBN 0 285 65093 9

Printed and bound in Great Britain by
The Guernsey Press Co. Ltd,
Guernsey, Channel Islands

Photoset by Rowland Phototypesetting Ltd,
Bury St Edmunds, Suffolk

I dedicate this book to my wife Sheila
who, since I met her, has always been
and continues to be the reason why
I do anything at all.

He looks at how it is and asks why?
I look at how it could be and ask why not.

Martin Luther King

Contents

Acknowledgements

To
Alan Tyne
without whom I would not have been able
to understand this book, much less
write it

Also to:

Chris Newall
Pat Dolan
Tom Dolan
Jean Hallworth
Julie Pogson
Karen Cumston
Cherly Sharp
Phillip Hallsworth
Kathy McGuire
Maggie Swindles
Mike Farragher
Hannah Forrest
Chris Gathercole
Cliff Cunningham
Eileen Clark
Hazel McKendrick
Louise Doulson
Gwenneth Skaife
Christine Beswick
Gaynor Drummond
Madeline Massey
Tracey Nichols

Hazel Quinn
Sue Thomas
Liz Farragher
Karen Walker
Jenny Smalley
Leslie Frost
Lizzie White
Martin Bibby
Tracey Doody
Howard Fox
Martin Forrest
Sue Lean
Joe Whittacker
Dane Pogson
Gerry Clark
Steve Tyler
Val Bindotti
Sonya Brown
Barbra Clancey
Paula Whittacker
Thorla Langley
Sylvia Elthorpe

Mary Hubbard
Kevin Reeves
Vivian Perry
Geoff Barnett
Pauline Bibby
Brenda Purvis
Michael Best
Colin McDonald
Ann Brown
Alistair Farragher
Clare Dolan
Cheryl Lean
Brian Eckersly
Mark Vaughan
Chris Rogerson
Heather Wyers
Camilla Stuart
Judith Lute
Susan White
Pauline Raymond
Heather Dewar
Sydney Bailey

Kath Goodall
Lorna Forrest
Alena Fleetwood
Lynn Barnett
Dennis Bibby
Carol Sampson
Michael Merrick
Sarah Barnett
Sue Barker
Alex Walker
Kate Palmer
Lauren Perry
Tricia Sloper
Andrew Taylor
Lynda Dodd
Joyce Jones
Linda Best
Colin Elliott
Jane Bowden
Jean Derby
Judy Lee
Brenda Kyle

xii *Acknowledgements*

Mich Hutchinson   John Jones   David Brandon   Sally Edmunds
North West Regional Health Development Team
Hester Adrian Research Centre—Manchester University
Stockport Education Authority
Centre for Studies on Integration in Education

Foreword

Excluding anyone from the mainstream of life always strikes us as wrong—so much so that we feel we have to justify it whenever it happens. So society sanctions the exclusion of some people, for some of the time, for some very clear reasons. It may be because they have committed a crime, or because they have an infectious illness, or simply because they are not in possession of the 'right papers'. But always, exclusion is accompanied by a lot of questioning, a lot of scrutiny.

Is it really necessary?

What kinds of guarantees and safeguards should we be offering to the excluded person?

How long will it last?

What are the conditions for being allowed back?

Whenever anyone is excluded, we all have a vested interest in questioning why and making sure the answers we get are really valid; otherwise, how are we to know that it will not be our turn next, or perhaps the turn of somebody we know and love? When exclusion is practised by a totalitarian state, or an obviously wicked regime, we can all see that it is wrong. Even though it will be 'justified', we all know the reasons given do not ring true and that in reality it is quite unjust. But when we practise exclusion ourselves we may be a little more inclined to accept the 'justifications', whatever the weaknesses in the argument. When trained and salaried professionals tell us, 'It's the only way,' 'They prefer it like this,' 'We can help them better,' or even, 'It isn't really exclusion,' the arguments seem even more persuasive, and we may be inclined to ignore the instincts that tell us exclusion is never really right and always has to be scrutinised most carefully. Sometimes the issues seem so complicated and technical that, as laypeople, we may feel unqualified to judge. What we see is a child who doesn't share the day-to-day experience of school with her brothers and sisters, her friends and neighbours. We see a family cut off from many of the normal experiences (both painful and pleasurable) of child rearing, and learning to regard their child as 'different', not just in respect of a particular disability, but in all aspects of her life. We see a young person growing into adulthood in a separate world, largely cut off from the ordinary experiences of others, and set on a path of perpetual separateness. We know this is wrong, but we may not recognise the sheer injustice it involves. Conversely, we may see it very clearly but be filled with resignation rather than the anger that other kinds of exclusion arouse in us.

The world of education has become a complex and technical one. Many ordinary people look at what goes on in schools today and marvel when they remember the schools of their youth. Some changes we all welcome, but others seem puzzling and appear to have very little to do with the common experience of the world outside. When people see the exclusion of a child, 'for sound educational reasons,' and feel uncomfortable about it, they may find it hard to question these reasons, as they would if they saw the same child being treated so differently by his friends and family. Although, in the wider world, the exclusion of disabled people from many aspects of ordinary life is increasingly challenged, this is rarely so in the world of education. Challenging, in any case, is never an easy or natural thing to do, particularly when people mean well and are working hard, trying to do their best. To challenge special schools and their teachers to examine thoughtfully what they are doing, and what consequences it will have on the lives of young people, might seem almost discourteous, or disloyal.

Maybe there's another reason, too, why challenging the practice of 'special' education can seem difficult. Teachers are mostly concerned with children who grow older and move on from their classes. There is perhaps less reason for them to question the rightness of what is done in special, exclusive and separate education, since it can be harder for them to see the longer-term consequences. Nevertheless, most teachers and educational administrators would recognise the dangers of a system in which assumptions were not challenged, established practices scrutinised, or the wider context of their work examined.

Kenn Jupp set out to examine, test, and challenge the limits of the system in which he found himself. As he explored these limits, he came across many helpful ideas in the wider world of the movements of disabled people and of people with learning difficulties in particular. He learned from parents of children with handicaps and built strong alliances with them as they worked together for change. The book he has written is an account of the learning journey they all went on together. It describes how they tackled their task with energy, comradeship and humour. They showed that genuine inclusion of children with substantial learning difficulties into the same schools and classrooms as their brothers and sisters, and their neighbours and friends, is perfectly practical. It can be done by ordinary people. There are no major problems of resources (time, money, skills, co-operation). The most important change needed is *in the way we think about children with substantial handicaps and about their families.*

The struggle for inclusion is going on all around us. People are no longer content (if they ever were) to accept exclusion from the opportunities in the mainstream of life. This book tells an exciting story of the ways in which our schools can support the inclusion of children with substantial handicaps into the lives of our communities. It shows, too, how doing this enriches the lives of the children, their families, the schools and their teachers and the communities they serve.

Alan Tyne
Founder, Community and Mental Handicap Research
Association (CMHERA).
Lifelong campaigner for people with
learning difficulties.

Part One

SPECIAL EDUCATION— THE NEED FOR CHANGE

1 A World of Difference

When it comes to planning human services, we often appear to be obsessed by what I can only describe as a bizarre compulsion to group people together. What is more, the criterion we use to select these groups is usually that they share just one common feature among them. Take age, for instance. Those over a certain age we collectively label 'geriatric' and proceed to accommodate them with other similarly elderly people in what become known as 'homes'. As a result, the word 'homes' it should be noted, quickly takes on a rather different connotation from the homes in which the rest of us live.

Then there are the people whom we group together primarily because they are unable to walk. These we refer to as 'the physically handicapped' or, even worse, 'PHs', and we provide them with 'hostels' in which to live with others who, like themselves, have limited mobility.

In addition to these, there are the people who fail to attain the sometimes very precise goals we set in respect of intellectual abilities. These we regard as having 'severe learning difficulties', and they too begin to lose their identity as individuals when we use short-hand and talk of them as 'SLDs' or 'the mentally handicapped'. Consequently they are brought together into yet another of our artificially manufactured groups, are housed with others who have a learning difficulty and are kept largely at arm's length from the rest of society.

It is strange, too, that once we have organised those who have special needs into these obscure groups, whether they be people who are elderly, those who are physically disabled or those who have a learning difficulty, we often expect them to live their lives in hospitals, cared for by nurses and doctors, despite the fact that they are not ill at all. Alternatively, we make available to them places which accommodate as many as twenty-five or more residents at any one time and call these 'units' or 'nursing homes' as opposed to 'houses'. Yet again, more often than not, these will be situated at a discreet distance from where the majority of the community is living—the majority being, presumably, those of us who are able to walk, are not too old and can achieve at least a mean score on a recognised standardised intelligence test.

In South Africa, as we know, that singular aspect of a person which is used to determine where he lives, what he does and with whom has traditionally been decided not so much by his degree of physical ability, his age or his learning capability, but rather by the pigmentation of his skin. Let us be thankful that in the United Kingdom it is at least illegal for us to separate people according to their racial origins and, by the same token, we are beginning to appreciate the nonsense of generalising about people simply in relation to their gender. Why, then, in all other respects, do we insist on continuing to base our human service provision on just one aspect of a person, whether it be his or her age, mobility or intellect? Assembling people in this way is surely as unnatural and futile as insisting that those of us who have red hair should live on the opposite side of the road from those of us who have blond hair, or that people who are tall (say above six feet) should be housed separately from those who are short (below six feet.) There will always be some of us who are exactly six feet tall, so what place, one wonders, is there for them in the great scheme of things? People who find themselves in this position tend to be labelled 'borderline cases', as though it were somehow their fault for not fitting into the system that we have so carefully designed.

It has become obvious to many who are currently employed within human services, as it has to many who use these services, that whenever we insist upon drawing such arbitrary lines and planning in this way, there will always be those who do not fit into the categories we have so painstakingly allocated for them. The plain fact of the matter is that all of us, irrespective of who we are, whilst being individuals and having quite singularly different needs, actually have more in common with each other than we do differences. In consequence, whilst some of us will have some very specific needs, if we make the mistake of focusing entirely upon these in isolation from the fundamental needs which we all have as people, it will only serve unnecessarily to magnify our differences and alienate ourselves from each other. Whoever we are, it is important that we should see ourselves and be seen by others as people first, and consider any special needs we may have as purely secondary to this fact. So often we hear reference to 'mentally handicapped' children, as though their mental handicap were their most important feature. In the real world, the one which exists outside the classroom, a child is a child is a child . . .

These single criteria by which we choose to group people are surely all quite relative anyway. Look at age as an example. Unarguably there are degrees of age, and your own position in the age spectrum will determine whether you perceive others as being old or young. It will also determine how others see you. Placed in a group consisting entirely of teenagers, for instance, a thirty-five-year-old may well be considered quite elderly. The same thirty-five-year-old, however, placed among people of seventy-plus, will likely be thought of as a mere stripling.

The same principle, of course, applies in deciding where one stands in the spectrum of physical dexterity and again in the spectrum of learning ability. Let's face it, most of us do not need to look far in order to discover several other people who are more intellectually capable than ourselves—more than several perhaps. The well-known Monty Python sketch on our British class structure can easily be applied to our attitudes towards learning difficulty: 'I look down on him because I have a higher IQ than he has, but I look up to him . . .' and so on. In reality, then, all of us to some extent can be said to have a learning difficulty, whether we like to think of it in that way or not. Likewise, there will always be those who can jump higher, run faster, walk farther than we can. I, for one, would not be capable of taking Daly Thompson's gold medal away from him at the next Olympics. We have to accept that we all have some degree of physical disability; we are all to some extent disabled.

The services we plan, therefore, should surely cater for our fundamental needs as people, long before we begin to address any additional special needs we may have. This means that our services, whether they be for people who are elderly, those who have a physical disability or children who have a severe learning difficulty, should first of all be accessible within the community at large; they should be the same services that are used by everyone. If we expect others to benefit from them, they should be services which we would be happy to use ourselves. Remember, all of us at some time are likely to use at least one human service. When we achieve 'elderly' status (which after all seems preferable to the alternative) will we be content to use those services which we are making available to people who are elderly now? If not, then changes should be made.

I think it was Mao Tse-Tung who said that the longest journey begins with the first step. While this is undeniably true, the journey becomes considerably longer when one discovers that this first step has been taken in entirely the wrong direction. But the very first step should be the one which is taken in our own heads. It is an essential first step, the one which lays down our firm foundation, the step which is the vision of our philosophy and the pathway to our destination. It is the step which ensures that everyone will be journeying together and in the same direction. Thankfully, due to legislation introduced over the past ten years or so and the vision of some service planners (predominantly those within District Health Authorities and Social Services Departments) the development of a new generation of human services is starting to take into consideration the need to include people, whatever their special needs, in the mainstream of daily life. The 'Care In the Community' philosophy and the principles of Normalisation are beginning to bring about fresh understanding of the way in which human services need now to be delivered.

However, whereas District Health Authorities and Social Services Departments throughout the United Kingdom are in general grappling with the issues to provide community-based services, Local Education Authorities seem to have been suffering quite noticeably from the 'Ostrich Syndrome'. The Warnock Report, which came and went more than ten years ago now, brought to our notice some sound rationale on meeting the special educational needs of children within the auspices of their local mainstream schools. Sadly, in practice this seems to have had a minimal effect. The 1981 Education Act followed; it was born very weak, it died and was then buried without a proper funeral or even an obituary. They both seem to have been forgotten and are now being pushed farther into yesterday's background, in today's scramble to implement the National Curriculum, Local Financial Management and a host of other newly acquired responsibilities. Generally speaking, if Education Authorities are having any dialogue at all about the issues of integrating children who have severe learning difficulties into mainstream education, it is largely to debate in terms of 'should we?' despite the fact that it has been a legal requirement for some years. District Health Authorities and Social Services Departments, on the other hand, when it comes to fulfilling their obligations to provide ordinary housing and real jobs for people who have severe learning difficulties, are at least asking 'How can we?' and 'How soon?'

On the whole, throughout the United Kingdom the 1981 Education Act seems to have become little more than a missed opportunity significantly to reform our special education system. One reason for this may well be that some Education Officers within Local Education Authorities have become quite adept at examining the letter of the law and manipulating it in such a way that they can apply it to their own Authority's existing pattern of provision with the minimum of change, so that it will cause them little or no cost and inconvenience. Thus they are able to say that they have complied fully with their new legal duties, whilst the spirit of the Act for the most part becomes lost. If one were to ask most headteachers of special schools what significant changes had occurred since the implementation of the 1981 Education Act, I suspect that they would be hard pushed to find an answer. Of course, there would likely be a certain amount of tokenism taking place—that is to say, a few selected children might now be visiting a nearby mainstream school. This would be occurring for perhaps half a day or so each week, almost certainly in groups rather than individually, and it is most unlikely that these children would be attending the school in the area where they live, as their brothers and sisters do. 'Doing integration', as some schools refer to it, for a half-day each week falls somewhat short of the ideals expressed by the Warnock Report and its subsequent legislation. Integration cannot be 'done' on a Wednesday afternoon. A child cannot be a 'little bit' integrated any more than a woman can be a 'little bit' pregnant. Inclusive education must be a total concept. The word 'inclusion' would perhaps be more appropriate for us to use than 'integration'. Most disabled people I know do not want to be integrated—they simply want to be included.

On the whole, then, we choose to educate children who have a severe learning difficulty quite separately from other children. We do this in just the same way that we choose to house people who have a physical disability and those who are elderly—in a segregated fashion. The reason for this, I am given to understand, is that it is 'for their own protection'.

Strangely, those of us who plan human services rarely seem to ask the consumers of these services what they themselves require. The car industry spends literally millions of pounds on market research before producing a new model. Manufacturers ask those who purchase cars whether they prefer performance to comfort, what colour car they like best, if fuel economy is of prime importance to them, and a host of other related questions. They do this, of course, to discover what people want *before* they build their new model; after all, if they produced a vehicle that did not meet with drivers' needs or approval, then cars would be purchased elsewhere and their business would go to the wall. This is quite different, however, from the development of human services which seem to be provided without reference to those who will be using them. If people are unable to use a service or feel that it is not what they want, then, contrary to the commercial culture, it is the consumer who goes to the wall and the Local Authority that thrives.

Since we are social animals, it is important for us to interact with our peers and be part of our local community, and yet we deny this basic human need to whole groups of people. We continue to develop services which take people out of our society, and in some cases even have the arrogance to assess people to see if they are ready to live among us—people who have neither offended nor committed a crime. I am thankful that I did not have to go through any form of assessment myself, to see if I was ready to live in the community. I shudder to think what the result of that might have been! Even children, if they have a severe learning difficulty (or a moderate one, for that matter) we insist should be separated from the rest of us by being placed in different schools. The time has surely come for us to think again, radically to reappraise the way in which we deliver special education. Does it meet the special needs of children who have severe learning difficulties? Does it really prepare such children for a meaningful life with their family and friends? Does it even allow them to have friends?

We seem to live in a somewhat illogical world, one in which half the people are starving and the other half are trying to lose weight. Perhaps now, in the field of special education at least, it is a good time for us to stop and think again.

2 Why Not Integrate?

All children are automatically included as pupils of their local school, unless of course we prevent them from attending. Indeed, this is a legal requirement in the United Kingdom and parents can be prosecuted for refusing to send their child to school. So why is it that we choose to refuse mainstream school places to some children but insist on the attendance of others, and how did this whole notion of educational segregation first begin?

ATTITUDES

To answer this properly we need to examine our society's attitudes towards disability. Those who have a severe learning difficulty appear to be viewed by the rest in several different ways. Some people regard them quite simply as objects of ridicule, a hangover from the 'village idiot' concept of the Middle Ages. For these people they are the butt of jokes: instant humour, the source of a guaranteed quick laugh. Such people often tend to be rather insecure about their own abilities.

Others show great pity for those who are disabled, uttering phrases like, 'Poor thing', 'It's his mother I feel sorry for', and 'There but for the grace of God . . . ' These people seek to offer protection, presumably from the warped 'humour' of those mentioned above, and from more sinister individuals who try to exploit vulnerability. It is this attitude that leads people to say things like, 'But they like to be with their own kind', and 'Society can be so cruel'. Recently, a woman wrote to her local voluntary organisation about her son who was in his early twenties. On most days he attended an Adult Training Centre which was situated in a neighbourhood quite some distance from his home. On the day in question, however, he had gone to a cinema in his own locality and was by himself. His mother described how four youths set about him and dragged him into a nearby derelict building, then blocked the exit and proceeded to set the building on fire. Fortunately, her son escaped unscathed, but she made the point that 'Care in the Community' would render her son, and others like him, defenceless against predators like these, and concluded that he would be better protected behind the locked doors of a safe, well-run institution. This seems a rather strange logic, when you consider that it advocates the incarceration of innocent victims and allows perpetrators of such acts to roam freely. It also assumes, quite wrongly, that institutions are by their nature places of safety.

There are also people who regard those who have a learning difficulty as being in some way ill, often confusing those who have a mental illness with those who have a reduced intellectual ability. Members of the medical profession often seem to take this view and may become more interested in discovering syndromes which give their own names immortality than in the needs of the person concerned. Relating well to a person and developing some understanding of his or her daily needs seems less important to some doctors, nurses and therapists than mending a broken leg or operating on a damaged organ. In consequence, those who have a severe learning difficulty may be regarded as 'medical conditions'; they may be considered in need of 'treatment', 'medication' or 'therapy' of one kind or another. They may even be permanently hospitalised!

Parents, particularly, may see a son or daughter who has a learning difficulty as an eternal child. Perhaps they have been told by various professionals that their teenager has a mental age of say, five years (whatever that may mean) and they assume, not unreasonably, that he or she will always remain a child. A child, after all, should be easier to cope with than an adult. Children will always want their mums and dads, they will always be loving and show overt affection in the way that children do. It means, too, that parents can have the joy of a child forever, without adolescent complications like sex, illicit smoking, the fear of drug addiction, glue sniffing, unwanted pregnancy or any of the other dangers that threaten today's teenagers. The concept of an eternal five-year-old may seem infinitely preferable. This may explain why people in their middle age are still clutching teddy bears, having to blow out candles on a birthday cake, or wearing inappropriately childish clothes like white ankle socks and Alice bands. The fact is, whether he has learning difficulty or not, a teenage boy is more likely to be interested in teenage girls, pop music and fashionable clothes than he ever is in teddy bears.

Some people look upon those who have learning difficulties as a menace or a threat. They regard them as unpredictable and potentially violent, brand them as 'unlucky' and feel uncomfortable in their presence. They see them as likely to molest young children or commit criminal acts generally. The truth is that, in percentage terms, those who have a severe learning difficulty are rarely responsible for any of these acts, while in comparison, the rest of us seem to indulge in them all too frequently.

Finally and in contrast, there are those of us who take the 'holy innocent' view. Religious orders particularly see a seriously disabled person as specially smiled upon by God, a living blessing who throughout his or her life will be pure, virginal and entirely without sin. Twenty years in the field of special education, however, tell me that such 'living blessings' are liable to commit as many sins as the next person, given a reasonable opportunity.

This combination of prejudiced attitudes, which we as a society have developed over the years, has shaped the way in which we deliver all our human services today. It forms the foundation of the educational apartheid that we live with at this moment. These attitudes are now so engrained that Local Education Authorities seem highly cautious of any attempt to include children who have severe learning difficulties in a mainstream school setting. Such attempts they say, must be closely monitored and regularly evaluated in detail. The same high degree of caution does not seem to apply to the child who remains in a segregated special school. The status quo, it seems, can be maintained without the same stringent account-ability. So, in most places, we continue to separate children 'for their own good', to prevent them being the *object of ridicule* of other children who, because they attend a different school in a different place and are taught by different teachers, not

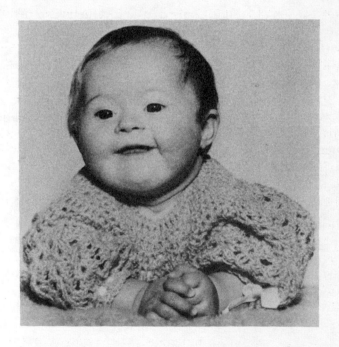

Object of ridicule? Holy innocent? Menace? Eternal child? Diseased organism? Object of pity? How do you see this child?

surprisingly see them as very different people. This perceived 'difference' forms the basis of attitude for future generations who learn to regard those who have a learning difficulty as *objects of pity, objects of ridicule, eternal children, menaces, diseased organisms* or *holy innocents*. And so the circle of ignorance is perpetuated.

THE ORIGIN OF SEGREGATED EDUCATION

In the United Kingdom, prior to 1971, those children whom we now describe as having severe learning difficulties were regarded as ineducable. Such children were exempt from attending school and the Local Education Authorities had no responsibility to make provision for them. Consequently, many remained at home all day with their parents who received little or no support. Health Authorities did, however, make provision for some, by means of establishments called junior training centres. These were staffed largely by para-medics within a caring/nursing rather than educational environment. The medical model was predominant and such services as existed were developed largely from a *diseased organism* attitude. By April 1971 the climate of opinion had begun to change, thanks to a growing feeling that no child was ineducable. An Act of Parliament transferred the responsibility for these children, who were then called severely subnormal, from Health Authorities to Local Education Authorities. Most Education Authorities were overwhelmed by their task and were at a loss to know how children of this degree of intellectual ability would fit in to their carefully constructed education system. The notion of comprehensive education did not stretch to this! The closest experience any educationalist had of children with special needs like this was with those who had a moderate learning difficulty (then referred to as educationally subnormal children). Education administrators were anxious: education, after all, meant teachers and classrooms and blackboards; these children had none of these! Education Authorities had for years put effort and resources into identifying those children who had moderate learning difficulties, in order to remove them from mainstream schools and place them in separate special schools. So the thought of children who had severe learning difficulties attending their local mainstream school was inconceivable. If anyone *had* conceived it, they would surely have been laughed at. The Local Education Authorities' solution, as always with an Act of Parliament like this, was to take the course of least resistance. Junior training centres were renamed special schools and paramedics, along with some unqualified staff, became teachers. The 1971 Education Act added 'educationally subnormal (severe)' to the growing list of categories that legally excluded children from being able to attend their local mainstream school. These categories were for children who were:

blind
partially sighted
deaf
partially hearing
delicate
physically handicapped
epileptic
maladjusted
educationally subnormal (moderate)
speech defects

Provision then was made for these children from attitudes that wanted to give protection. Provision was designed to protect *objects of pity, diseased organisms, eternal children* and *objects of ridicule*. Such provision was to be 'special'. It was to be carried out in a special place by special teachers with special equipment. Non-disabled children, too, were protected from the *menace* of those who had special needs.

WHAT IS SO SPECIAL ABOUT SPECIAL SCHOOLS?

The Building
Have special schools really changed that much since they were known as junior training centres? Even the briefest look inside

shows us that the bricks and mortar themselves are not very different from those of any other school. They have an assembly/PE/dining hall like most other primary schools. Classrooms, a head's office, staff room and caretaker's room are more or less the same, too. Perhaps the better resourced special schools will have their own, in-house swimming pool, but in its design this is unlikely to differ much from the community swimming pool that the rest of us use. So, purely in building terms, there seems to be no difference between a special school and a mainstream school. In most cases, if the special school were made empty, it would be relatively easy to transfer the children from the local primary school into it, and vice versa.

Staffing Ratio

Many children are referred to special schools on the understanding that they will receive one-to-one attention. This is a misconception shared by many people. Of course, special schools are given a 'most favourable' teaching ratio, which seems to average at around one teacher for every six or seven children. Some Education Authorities are more generous, but many are considerably worse. In real terms, one-to-one teaching for a child who has severe learning difficulties, will mean sharing a teacher with five or six others, all of whom have severe learning difficulties. Since these children will have very individual special educational needs, it is rarely possible to teach them effectively in groups. Consequently, due to demands that will undoubtedly be placed on the class teacher by classmates, in practice individual tuition can usually be only infrequent, and for short periods.

Poor Models of Learning

When admitted to a special school that caters primarily for those who have a severe learning difficulty, it is inevitable that children with speech difficulties will be grouped with others who also have problems of communication. How do we expect such children to develop communication skills when they are unable to hear and see good standards going on? I suspect that if we were to place a baby with no special needs (if there is such a baby!) in a special school where the infant, on a daily basis saw little attempt by others to communicate and heard little in the way of spontaneous, regular, consistent speech, then such a child, by the time he was four or five years old, would also have serious language delay. Similarly, our special schools only accommodate children who have a range of needs, such as challenging behaviour or poor social skills, or perhaps high dependency. This presents very little opportunity for any child to witness good models and in general creates a poor learning environment.

Difficulties for the Teacher

In the final analysis, it is the class teacher who is left with the problem of coping with the sheer logistics in meeting the special educational needs of those children within the class. Usually, she is presented with:

    a room or area in which to base the class
    access to a range of equipment
    the assistance of another adult
    a time-share in the school's minibus
    a time-share in the assembly hall

In the normal course of events, this provision would be quite adequate. However, given that the class is composed entirely of children who have severe learning difficulties, it is easy to understand that these resources may not only be regarded as insufficient to meet individual special needs, but in some circumstances may be quite counter-productive. For example, taking a class for swimming lessons will necessitate them dressing and undressing. This is an important social skill which they should be learning to accomplish for themselves. The swimming lesson, of course, provides an excellent opportunity for them to learn this skill in an appropriate context. With a class of seven children, however, and under the constraints of time (to ensure that the group following is not kept waiting, or perhaps to get back to school in time for lunch or the next allocated activity) one can begin to see how the needs of the individual child, which we attempt to hold paramount, become eroded and begin to assume a lesser priority in competition with our own administrative needs and daily routines.

Similar difficulties are found even where teaching takes place in the classroom itself. Each child in a special school will be at a differing level of ability in each of the key areas of the curriculum. Levels of attainment in communication, mathematics, science, social skills and physical development will probably be markedly different for every child in the class and will bear little relationship to their chronological age. Situations in which such a group can learn effectively together are few and far between and, for the most part, individual tuition will be necessary. There being only one teacher to six or seven children, it follows that her task becomes extremely difficult, to say the least.

Problems Created by Extended Catchment Areas
Since children who are referred to special schools come from all over the area designated the responsibility of the Local Education Authority, it follows that special schools will invariably have a far wider catchment area than any mainstream school. This always creates a number of disadvantages, most of which seem to be centred around transport.

1   Home/school liaison, an extremely important consideration for families whose children have learning difficulties, cannot easily be fostered where distance is a factor.

2   Some very young severely disabled children will spend up to two hours each day, and sometimes more, travelling to and from school. Pre-school-aged children in general, who do *not* have a disablement, would not normally be expected to cope with this.

3   Some parents find it very difficult to collect one child from their mainstream school and at the same time be at

home to receive their child who attends the special school. At least one Education Authority, to my knowledge, has a policy that transport contractors should only wait for *two minutes* if parents are not at home to receive their child. After that, the child should be taken directly to the police station or to the town hall.

4   Transport has become a significant financial consideration for Local Education Authorities since it now represents the single most costly resource (with the exception of teachers' salaries) provided in special schools.

It would seem that getting children to and from special schools in this way is not only excessively expensive, but also counter-productive to the children's special needs and to those of their families. The children themselves miss out on the experiences that their brothers and sisters have when they walk to school at the top of the road each day, and their parents become more isolated from other parents who live locally and who accompany their children to school.

THE IMMORALITY OF A SEGREGATED SYSTEM

The mark of a civilised society is that it supports its weakest member, rather than following its strongest. If we subscribe to the belief that people who have learning difficulties should take their place in the community and are entitled to the same choices, opportunities and status that the rest of us enjoy, then it seems to make very little sense for us to create abnormal experiences and environments during their childhood and school years by segregating them from other children. A deaf child, after all, will be living in a hearing world and a physically disabled child in a mobile one.

In our bid to protect children who have special needs, by sheltering them within special establishments, we inevitably, even if unwittingly, discriminate against them. In recent years Local Educational Authorities have started to become more aware of multiracial and multicultural issues within schools, along with issues of gender. When I was at school, most establishments catered either for girls or boys, but not for both. Where co-education existed, boys and girls were made to use different playgrounds. Not so long ago in the United States, the same sort of segregation took place on the basis of skin colour. In the United Kingdom now, there would undoubtedly be an outcry if blacks were made to attend different schools from whites, or if they were compelled to eat at special tables or were kept in a special class or unit away from other children in the school. The choice of local school that is given to most parents is not afforded to parents of children who have severe learning difficulties. These children, we say, must be segregated into special schools 'for their own good'.

Our society uses numerous euphemisms to make the unpalatable sound more acceptable. 'Asylums for the insane,' became 'psychiatric hospitals', 'wards in subnormality hospitals', became 'villas', and now we have 'special schools'. This conveys to people the idea that the school is in some way specially beneficial and advantageous quite different from all other run-of-the-mill schools. It creates the notion that the building itself is special and utterly unlike all other school buildings, so that it can accommodate special children in particular. And what is inside these special schools? Why, special teachers, of course, who have special teaching methods and special educational equipment which somehow prepares special pupils, at school leaving age, to be launched into the real world outside where they can live more meaningfully and independently than they otherwise would. Strange that we have to take them *from* the real world outside to do this. I suppose it is easy to think of children who have special needs in terms of protection, but it is important that we examine closely our true motives. Segregation, after all, is a two-way process. Adolf Hitler segregated the Jews, those who had a disability and homosexuals from other Germans, in order to protect the master race from 'impurities'. South Africa segregated its blacks in order to protect its whites. When it comes to segregating those who have special needs, we should not flinch from asking ourselves who it is that we are attempting to protect.

Once a child has been identified as having severe learning difficulties, we can be fairly confident about the route which that child will be destined to take throughout the system of future provision that will be made available to him. Having attended a special school all through his childhood, he will most likely attend an adult training centre. Often, however, a place is unavailable, in which case he or she will stay at home all day, looked after by parents. Those who take up a place in the adult training centre (or Social Education Centre, as some are called) will be destined to spend the rest of their lives in this establishment. The word 'training' in adult training centre is often confusing, since it is unclear what people are being trained for. It is surely not for a job, since very few 'trainees' actually leave the centre to go into open employment. Not all youngsters go into adult training centres directly from special school of course. Some attend a college of further education for two years; then they go into an adult training centre, or remain at home. Sooner or later, due to the death or total fatigue of those who care for them, most people who have severe learning difficulties will end up living in a place provided by the District Health Authority or Social Services Department. This will take the form of a hospital, a twenty-four bedded unit or, for those most fortunate, a group home, which will be either supported or unsupported.

With the exception perhaps of group homes, the majority of residential provision will mean that people who have learning difficulties will be cared for by medical and paramedical staff or social workers, or both. They are likely to have little choice about what they wear, what they eat, where they go on holiday, who they live with, what furniture and décor they are surrounded by. They will have little privacy, few hobbies, even fewer real friends and will be accountable for almost everything they do. Whilst most Health Authorities and Social Services Departments are these days aware of these flaws in the provision they make available, they have as yet only been able to develop more ideal support for a minority.

As things stand, equal opportunity is not something that people who have a severe learning difficulty can realistically expect, either during their school years or in adulthood. After leaving their special school, we can with some degree of reliability predict the way in which their lives will continue to be severely limited in opportunity, status and just about everything else. They are destined to be restricted in the same way as someone serving a prison sentence, although they have committed no crime and will not qualify for remission. The field of special education seems full of nice people doing terrible things quite unintentionally. They build sparkling new special schools which will only serve further to incarcerate, no matter how well resourced they may be. Raising funds to provide any special equipment or facility, when it can perfectly well be provided in the ordinary way, will only serve to exclude people and deny them the opportunities and experiences that the rest of us seem able to take for granted. Anything which highlights the differences between us will only take away from the overwhelming sameness that we share with one another.

Why not integrate and bring normality into what are said to be the best years of people's lives?

3   The Statement of Special Educational Needs—But Whose Needs?

More than a decade has passed since the Warnock Committee met and expressed the view that *all* children should have the opportunity to go to their local school. This sentiment even made it as far as the statute books in the form of the 1981 Education Act, since which time Local Education Authorities seem to have gone to great lengths to ensure that the right-sounding phrases appeared throughout their various policy documents, but really not much more when it came to the plight of those children who have severe learning difficulties. I hope I do not sound too paranoid when I say that sometimes there seems almost to be a conspiracy among professionals to prevent these children from learning alongside their local friends and neighbours. Some educational psychologists, for instance, will go out of their way to explain that a particular child needs to learn in a small group, as though for some mysterious reason this can only be provided within the confines of a special school.

The 1981 Education Act is quite clear: it states that all children should attend their local mainstream school unless:
- a) they themselves would suffer by doing so;
  or
- b) they would cause other children in the local mainstream school to suffer;
  or
- c) it would not be regarded as an efficient and economic use of resources.

The last proviso mentioned is, I am sure, a great favourite with the bureaucrats. This same Act demands that those children who are thought to have special educational needs must, in their own interest, have a written statement which lays down individually detailed information regarding their specific needs and the provision the Local Education Authority proposes to make, in order to meet these needs. To ensure that a comprehensive knowledge of the child's needs is obtained, a report from everyone who has been associated with the child is sought. Usually this will mean written assessments and recommendations from parents, teachers, an educational psychologist, a medical officer and perhaps paramedical staff such as a physiotherapist, an occupational therapist, a speech therapist and a health visitor, where necessary. Once all these written reports have been completed, they are sent to a named officer, employed by the Local Education Authority, whose task it is to read them, summarise them and produce a simple statement declaring the child's needs, the proposed provision and where the child should be educated. This is formulated from advice which is contained within all the written recommendations that the officer has collected.

The 1981 Education Act states that this whole process should take no longer than six months; however, few Education Authorities in practice seem to achieve this. A period of nine months appears to be more usual and eighteen months is by no means unheard of. As one parent said to an education officer, 'It seems that it is quicker to give birth to a baby than to write a statement of special needs!' Of course, there is nothing to prevent parents from obtaining written reports and recommendations themselves, by privately engaging any professionally qualified person of their choice, either on a voluntary or fee-paying basis. An educational psychologist, perhaps, or a physio or speech therapist. All these reports have to be taken into account by the named person, and parents must be given full copies of every report written about their child, whoever writes them, whether they be engaged by the parents themselves or are employed by the Education or Health Authority.

More than that, in fact, for all parents have the right to be in attendance when their child's needs are being assessed by anyone who is contributing to the statement.

The statement itself is simple enough. It is divided into five sections, with the written reports forming the appendices:

Section One: gives simple details of the child's name and address, date of birth, etc.

Section Two: states what special educational needs the child has.

Section Three: states what provision the Education Authority intends to make, in order to meet these stated needs.

Section Four: indicates where the child's special educational needs are to be met.

Section Five: states what non-educational special needs the child has.

Whatever is written in Sections Two and Three forms the basis of a legally binding contract. It is perhaps not surprising, then, that some Local Education Authorities are somewhat sparse and indistinct in what they write within these sections. I have known some children in the past, whose disabilities have included epilepsy, quadriplegia, blindness, and deafness, which obviously have caused them to develop quite complex needs. Despite this, Sections Two and Three of their statements had each been completed with just one simple sentence. The following is an example:

Section Two: Janet has considerable physical and sensory handicaps and as such has the needs of a profoundly handicapped child.

Section Three: Janet should have an individual curriculum such as those that exist within a school for children with severe learning difficulties.

Statements like this may seem a godsend to many parents, but in fact they tell us nothing and merely pay lip service both to the spirit of the 1981 Education Act and to the child's needs.

Our present special education system allows for little choice. Young children identified as having a severe learning difficulty, whether through developmental delay or pre/peri/post-natal trauma, are rarely given any option but to be placed on the register of a special school, making many statementing procedures rather a foregone conclusion. From the age of two years and sometimes even younger, children, along with their parents, are sent from such places as child development clinics to special schools in order to view them. Many parents arrive at the school in an anxious and often confused state, totally unaware what their rights are; what a statement is; what options are open to them; what procedures are likely to take place.

A considerable number of parents, in my experience, particularly those whose children have already been attending their local playgroup, do not want their child to attend a school miles from their own neighbourhood and suddenly to be separated from the friends they have made locally. Nor do they want them to be segregated into an environment where all the other children in their class will have significant special needs. These parents are particularly concerned that their son or daughter will be deprived of good models of learning and only have poor examples of behaviour to copy. They feel that their child is being unnecessarily separated from other children right from the very beginning of his or her childhood and educational life, and excluded from the everyday events, routines and experiences that other children are able simply to take for granted.

By the same token, other parents have an expectation of special facilities being made available to meet their childs' needs, just because they have become conditioned by the fact that special needs are always met in this way; they assume that segregation is the most beneficial and appropriate course to follow, as this will provide special facilities which are essential for their child's development and well-being.

By the time their son or daughter has been designated as having special educational needs, many parents have been through the various systems of referral, on a roller-coaster of confusion and contradictions. They will have met a plethora of professionals, some of whom have been insensitive, some who have been vague and some who have been unashamedly inaccurate with their information. Special schools, for example, always seem to have quite a number of teenage youngsters who, their parents report, were not expected by the professionals to survive beyond two years of age. To many parents, professionals, like the Pope, are infallible. After all, they are so highly paid and it takes months for whole teams of them to complete a statement of a child's needs, so how can they be wrong? Frequently, because parents are not given a clear understanding of their entitlements, they accept opinions and provisions made by professionals as being absolute and put little value upon their own thoughts and judgements. For those Education Authorities who seek to put their own financial and administrative needs before the special educational needs of the child, parents in this situation can be sitting ducks!

Whilst parents may be told the rudiments of procedure about their child's statement of needs, they rarely appreciate how this same statement can be used, like a funnelling tool, to ensure their child's admission into a segregated special school, if this happens to be the cheapest and most convenient option for the Authority. Whilst schools for children who have severe learning difficulties continue to exist, Local Education Authorities will always find children who have severe learning difficulties with whom to fill them. This, despite the fact that the 1981 Education Act quite definitely and completely abolished all categories of disability. Gone forever, says the Act, are references to categories, for these tell us very little. Now we must focus our attention upon the child's individual needs and use our combined resources to meet them. From 'idiots, imbeciles and feeble minded', one Act of Parliament after another in its own enlightened way changed terminology to be redefined as 'severely subnormal' and then 'educationally subnormal (severe)'. At last we are confronted with legislation which does away with all labels in favour of personal need, and what do we do? We capture this whole concept in yet another fatuous label of SLD, which we use to describe 'a rose by any other name'. For as long as special schools continue to exist and cater for a particular category of disability, no matter what label we attach to it, such categories will never be truly abolished and we shall carry on failing to meet the special educational needs of individual children.

Educational psychologists, too, can be placed in the impossible position of being able to offer just one facility—a special school. Whilst Local Education Authorities do not dictate to educational psychologists what to recommend in their reports, it is by no means unknown for them to constrain psychologists, by preventing them from naming specific equipment, or from delineating actual amounts of classroom support time. How does the statement so often serve to ensure that children are placed in special schools as opposed to being adequately supported within their own local mainstream school? We only have to read one typical statement to get the answer. Let us take Malcolm as an example and read the statement that was prepared for him.

Malcolm's parents had approached their Local Education Authority and asked for their son to receive support to attend the same local mainstream school as his sister and friends, instead of continuing to go to his special school which catered only for children who had severe learning difficulties. This school, the parents maintained, was a considerable distance from where Malcolm lived and the children in his class were considerably more disabled than he was, which meant that he heard very little speech. After a great deal of procrastination from various officers within the Authority and a quite concerted effort by them to dissuade the parents from this course of action, Malcolm's parents insisted that their son should undergo a restatementing of his needs. This meant written advice being given about Malcolm's needs by his teachers, an educational psychologist and all those who knew him. The following statement of his needs was the result.

Section Two (special educational needs):
    Malcolm is a Down's Syndrome child who needs a high level of individual attention. Malcolm needs a Developmental Learning Programme. He attends ★★★★★★★★★★★★ school for children who have severe learning difficulties.

Section Three (provision to meet these needs):
    Malcolm should attend a school for children with severe learning difficulties, which can provide a Developmental Curriculum.

Section Four (appropriate school or other arrangements):
    Malcolm should continue to attend ★★★★★★★★★★★★ school.

Section Five (additional non-educational provision):
    Regular speech therapy and continued occupational therapy support.

Let us examine Section Two in more detail. 'Malcolm is a Down's Syndrome child', it states, as though this should be regarded as having some significance. Since people who have Down's Syndrome vary from each other as much as people who have driving licences do, this tells us nothing about Malcolm's special educational needs. The Down's Children's Association once made this point by displaying a poster of a toddler who had Down's Syndrome. Underneath the caption read, 'You call him Mongol, we call him Down's Syndrome.' It then went on to say, 'His friends call him David.'

    Section Two goes on to say that Malcolm 'needs a high level of individual attention.' This, of course, is not in fact a need, but a provision, and would have done better to appear in Section Three. More to the point, it does not indicate to us what Malcolm requires a high level of individual attention for.

'Malcolm needs a Developmental Learning Programme,' continues the statement. Again this is a provision, not a need. It does not tell us *why* he needs a Developmental Learning Programme, or what it would accomplish. Furthermore, it is meaningless jargon, or perhaps I should say, a coded phrase which is used and understood by professionals to mean that Malcolm is destined for a place within a school for children who have severe learning difficulties. Similarly, the terms 'Modified Curriculum' and 'Modified Learning Programme' are used by professionals to spell out placement within a school for children who have moderate learning difficulties. So far, we have barely got through the first part of Malcolm's statement and have certainly learned nothing about his special educational needs, yet his school placement has, in effect, already been determined.

Section Two concludes, 'He attends ★★★★★★★★★★★★ school for children, who have severe learning difficulties. Yet again, this tells us nothing of Malcolm's special educational needs, but certainly strengthens the Education Authority's bid to keep Malcolm exactly where he is.

We move on then to Section Three of the statement (special educational provision), having up to now learned nothing of Malcolm's needs. 'Malcolm should attend a school for children with severe learning difficulties which can provide a Developmental Curriculum,' it hammers home, closing the net as tightly as it can.

Section Four (appropriate school or other arrangements) of course read, 'Malcolm should continue to attend ★★★★★★★★★★★★ school.' Game, set and match to the Education Authority! The status quo has been maintained. The law has been complied with, justice has been seen to be done and all with the minimum of inconvenience and cost to the Authority. Its needs as an Authority have been perfectly well met.

Finally, the cream on the cake, the jewel in the crown. Section Five reads, 'Regular speech therapy and continued occupational therapy support.' The Education Authority is quite safe here. Since these therapies are not primarily its responsibility, it cannot be made to provide them. Neither can the District Health Authority, for that matter, as this part of the statement is not legally enforcible. However, just to make quite sure, the phrase that is used is careful not to elaborate on the specific frequency intended by the words 'regular' and 'continued'. In fact, Malcolm sees an occupational therapist once a year and a speech therapist about once every six weeks. Parents do, of course, have the right to appeal against their child's statement, but in practice they need to be emotionally strong, persistent and well informed to have any chance of success. For the most part, they are left with feelings of total frustration and fatigue.

Parents simply want some choice in their child's educational provision. They need to have confidence in a service that will address the special needs of the individual and will put those needs uppermost. They should also be able to have real influence in determining service provision, but in reality this rarely seems to happen. Both the Warnock Committee and the 1981 Education Act referred to parents as a vital source of information, experience and expertise that should be harnessed in equal partnership with professionals in order to achieve the best for their sons and daughters. Alas, in practice, many parents feel intimidated and devalued. A request for their child to attend the local mainstream school like their brothers and sisters is too often interpreted as evidence that they have not yet accepted their child's disability. If they persist, merely wanting some normality in their child's life, they are likely to be regarded as neurotic, emotionally fragile and slightly unbalanced. One of the primary aims of the 1981 Education Act was to encourage Local Education Authorities to make educational provision within the mainstream of education for children who have special needs. It was a significant bid to include, in schools at least, those pupils who up until now have been quite definitely excluded. The statement of special needs was designed to assist us to see how this could be done. What a nonsense it is, then, that we are still debating whether children who have severe learning diffi-culties should attend their local school when it has been their statutory right for eight years or more. Surely it would be far more appropriate for us to be discussing what it would take to support such children in their local mainstream schools and how we might go about it. So many times I have heard professionals talk of providing a child with the 'protection' of a statement. The question must be asked: is it really the child who is protected, or the interests of the Education Authority? The statement, I fear, has become little more than a passport to segregated schooling, which in turn becomes a passport to a segregated life.

4 Closing Special Schools and Opening Opportunities

Our commitment to special schools, both financially and ideologically, is now so deeply entrenched that although the argument in favour of integrating children who have special needs make undeniably good sense, there is an almost immovable reluctance to abolish any of them. Even an Act of Parliament has really only led to a certain amount of tokenism. Just the mere suggestion of change is likely to set most people on their mettle, and now, more than ever before, our education system is experiencing a period of considerable reform. The onset of local financial management in schools: staff appraisal; implementation of the National Curriculum; a new role for school governors; schools opting out—surely these are enough to send the educationalists stampeding hot foot towards the nearest aspirin bottle, or so we would think. In fact, so far these changes seem to have met with a remarkably minimal amount of disquiet.

Set against this background, one could be forgiven for thinking that asking an Education Authority to absorb just one extra child, with additional support, into his or her local school would present little difficulty, but not so, it seems. Given that this child has a severe learning difficulty, a torrent of emotion is likely to be released both in favour of and against the proposals. Those against, who prefer to engage the traditional special services, are usually deeply concerned that such children will somehow lose out; whilst those who, like myself, are in favour of adopting an alternative, seem to be attempting to turn on its head the whole concept of special needs along with the provision we make. Whilst for some it may seem to be a question of whether we are throwing baby out with the bath-water, for others it becomes more a concern that we may well be leaving baby in the bath-water to drown.

Most Education Authorities have a policy which states that, wherever possible, children who have special needs will have these needs met within a mainstream school, but this usually turns out to be a hollow statement which is simply bandied around so that the Authority can be seen to comply with the 1981 Education Act. The words are rarely backed up by a detailed strategy with which to implement the policy. Indeed, whilst making this pronouncement, some Education Authorities even continue to plan and build brand new special schools.

There can be very little doubt that just about everyone holds a strong view on the subject of integration: parents, education officers, teachers in mainstream schools, teachers in special schools, psychologists, classroom assistants, councillors—in short, anyone who cares about the education of children. So where is the common ground? With what do we all agree? Well, everyone would surely want:

a)   Quality education for all.
b)   More choice within our education service.
c)   A flexible system of service delivery.
d)   Equal opportunity for all children.
e)   To meet satisfactorily the special educational
     needs of children who hold a statement.
f)   An efficient use of resources.

So how can we create an alternative system of special education, which meets all the above-mentioned criteria and is advantageous to everyone? In essence, I believe that the success of any scheme devised to integrate children is dependent upon three main considerations.

1 That the proportion of those who are to be included should be considerably smaller than that of the pupils with whom they are to be placed. Of many schools that currently cater exclusively for children who have severe learning difficulties, it is true to say that their complete closure would mean that all their children could be absorbed by mainstream schools within the same Authority at a rate of just one child for each school, or even less.

2 That both functional and locational integration is more likely to be successful initially where children have *severe* rather than *moderate* learning difficulties. Those who have severe learning difficulties usually engender positive discrimination by other children, whereas a child with a less obvious or hidden disability is more likely, perhaps, to become the target for ridicule. Children who have serious and obvious disablements seem to be more likely to find the force of group dynamics in their favour. That is not to deny that *all* children should be integrated into mainstream schools, for they most definitely should, but in order to achieve this it may be advisable to start the process with those children who are most disabled.

3 Finally, that adequate support be provided, for both the included child and the receiving school.

Most Local Education Authorities, whether it seems like it or not, spend huge amounts of money in providing special educational services. The sad fact is that the major proportion of this extensive financial commitment is not directly effective as far as the child with special needs is concerned, the very person whom it is intended to benefit. Staggering amounts are spent on just transporting children to and from their school. Paying out £1,500 for each child per academic year is by no means unusual for many Local Education Authorities, and yet there are probably more complaints received about transport than any other single aspect of special education. Ironically, transport is not only frequently counter-productive to the child's education, but is totally unnecessary once he or she attends the local school. So not only is a considerable amount of money saved, but so is a considerable amount of inconvenience and anxiety on the part of the child and his family. Likewise, if each child at present attending a special school for children who have severe learning difficulty were to attend the school that he or she would normally have attended, had we and our special services not prevented him from doing so, then a complete financial saving could be made on the special school itself.

Many costs like these which are attributed to a special school system are, it must be said, both expensive and in fact non-educational. A number of special schools, for instance, are, whether they realise it or not, paying out thousands of pounds each year, in interest alone, on money that was borrowed to build or convert them in the first place. Then we must consider the cost of maintaining both the school building and the grounds surrounding it, and of course, there is the outlay for lighting, heating, caretakers' salaries, cleaners' salaries, secretaries' salaries, telephone bills, poll tax, cooks and kitchen staff, cleaning materials, office equipment—the list is almost endless.

If we were to accumulate the savings from these costly and somewhat unnecessary commodities, we could start to finance an alternative special education system which would provide more direct and personalised support for children who have special needs. We would then be able to place these children in their local schools, each with their own full-time classroom assistant and an individually designed programme of activities. Added to this, we could provide a full-time specialist teacher (from the teaching staff of the now closed special school) for every six or seven children, or whatever number the teacher had had in her class in the special school. Then, instead of being faced with the difficulties and restrictions of teaching groups of severely disabled children in a

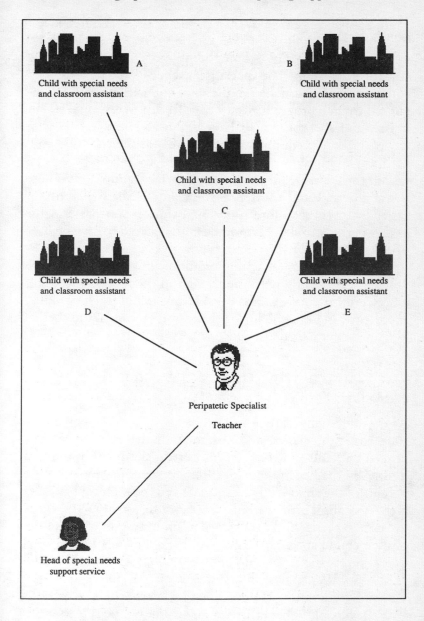

Figure 1. Network of support for children with special needs in mainstream schools.

confined space, she would still have six or seven children in her class, but each child would be attending his or her own local school and each child would be supported by a full-time classroom assistant. The specialist teacher would be in a much better position to use their experience and expertise in designing tailormade programmes of activity for every child in her 'class', and she could also have these activities carried out wherever they were most appropriate—at the child's home, the local swimming pool, a restaurant, on public transport, within the mainstream classroom—in fact, almost anywhere and at any time and as often as she wanted. She would find it easier to carry out more individual tuition sessions and for longer periods, and she would be better placed to give professional support and in-service training to the classroom assistants. The latter, meanwhile, would be in a good position to work in partnership with the teacher in the receiving school, who would also have a considerable amount of teaching skills, experience and knowledge of education to contribute. Let us look at the way such a scheme works in practice.

THE ROLE OF THE CHILD'S CLASSROOM ASSISTANT

As the child will be attending his or her local school on a full-time basis, the classroom assistant will also need to be employed on a full-time basis. This person should be appointed jointly by the headteacher of the mainstream school and the parents of the child who has special needs or their representative. After all, it is the parents who are most likely to have the greatest expertise and experience in understanding the nature of their child's special needs. The formal qualifications of such a classroom assistant should be regarded as less important than her personal qualities and abilities. She is likely to enjoy working with young children, have a warm friendly personality, be flexible in her attitudes and thinking, be able to work well in a team, be a good communicator, relate well to others and be able to learn quickly. If you think that such a paragon of virtue is impossible to come by, I should tell you that in Stockport we recently advertised such a post and received one hundred and twenty applications from which to choose.

For administrative purposes, this classroom assistant will be placed under the jurisdiction of the mainstream school's head-teacher and will adhere to the in-house rules of the school, following its daily routines like everyone else. In this way she will more easily be absorbed as part of the staff and integrated more effectively, like the child she is supporting. Whilst the classroom assistant should, of course, always be cognisant of the supported child's whereabouts and actions, it would not normally be a good idea to be constantly at his elbow. The skills of a classroom assistant in this situation are, broadly speaking, ones of awareness, a subtle presence, a knowledge of when and when not to intervene and an ability to blend in with the rest of the class. The way in which this is done will be dependent upon a number of factors, including the nature of the child's needs, the personality of the classroom assistant and the general ambiance of the school. The rapport that is shared between the classroom assistant and the class teacher is of paramount importance. Many class teachers in mainstream schools are not used to working with another adult, and some find this more threatening than taking on the special needs of the child. For this reason, it should be understood from the beginning that the classroom assistant is directly responsible to the mainstream school's class teacher and not to the visiting specialist teacher. It may well be that the class teacher will sometimes want the classroom assistant to work with small groups of children, groups that do not include the child with special needs, or to work in a completely different class or another part of the school. If this should be the case, so much to the good. What better evidence is there that the child has been completely integrated?

THE ROLE OF THE SUPPORTING SPECIALIST TEACHER

Initially, the specialist teacher will very likely be concentrating her efforts of support as much on the classroom teacher as on the child who has special needs. After all, class teachers, like the rest of us, are themselves the products of a segregated education and as such are likely to have coloured attitudes towards disability. This, coupled with an overall uneasiness about their own ability to cope, may lead to an unnecessarily tense atmosphere within the classroom, which could be detrimental to everyone. It is up to the specialist teacher to ensure that the receiving class teacher gains a proper perspective on the situation and is helped to understand that the new recruit is simply a child, made up in just the same way as any other; his special needs, however severe they may be, are purely a secondary factor. Class teachers often need to have their confidence boosted and shown that they have as much to contribute as the specialist teacher, if not more. Most of them, no matter how strung up they may be at first, usually relax once they have experienced the general normality of a child who has special needs. They will also begin to realise that there is really very little mystique in special education and that specialist teachers do not, in fact, have all the answers.

The specialist teacher must be supportive of the child, the child's parents, the classroom assistant, the class teacher and the headteacher of the receiving school. She should make it her business to get to know as many as she can of those who regularly come into contact with the supported child. These will include other children, caretakers, dinner ladies, school secretaries and anyone else who is likely to have some direct bearing on the child's school life. Their attitudes are just as important as those of the class teacher; those who are too sympathetic, over-protective, indulgent and pitying can be as much of a hindrance as those who are unco-operative and stand-offish.

Primarily, the responsibility of the specialist teacher is to work in partnership with the class teacher in each of the designated mainstream schools, together with the children's appointed classroom assistants and parents. Between them, they will be able to decide when and how best the child can be functionally integrated into the class. The existing timetable will probably form the basis for this initial discussion and will of course be a matter for continual evaluation. In the majority of schools, we can realistically expect most supported children, whatever their degree of disability, to take their place alongside the other children in the class, sharing such events as meal-times, physical education sessions, design and technology and so on. For some, though certainly not all, very formal lessons and activities with a high academic content may prove totally inappropriate, and in these circumstances the classroom assistant, or perhaps the visiting specialist teacher, can withdraw the child in order to give him individual tuition which has more relevance to his own specific needs.

Such withdrawal need not necessarily be restricted to another room in the school, although this could be one option. It should always be a positive action and can be implemented in numerous ways according to the demands of individual special needs. For example, withdrawal may mean that the classroom assistant accompanies the child to the local swimming pool with a small group of classmates, or perhaps for horse-riding lessons, or simply to visit local shops to learn money values and road sense. The specialist teacher may want to spend a session with the child at his home, working with the parents to teach a particular skill or concept *in situ*; or the time may be used to visit the physiotherapist or speech therapist—the options are limitless. Whatever activity is chosen, it must be properly planned by the specialist teacher in consultation with the others, so that these periods become useful opportunities for in-depth tuition.

Withdrawal, then, must always be used to introduce an activity which will be enjoyable, relevant, meaningful and particularly helpful to the child, rather than seen as a negative step which is taken merely to prevent classroom disruption.

For many supported children, withdrawal actually means staying in the same class and continuing with school-work at their own level, with assistance from an adult, while the other children carry on with their formal lesson. Under this alternative system of special education, both the mainstream and specialist teachers, together with the parents and classroom assistant, will have the opportunity to plan the child's active school day, decide just how and when individual or small group activities should take place and judge when the child should be withdrawn. The amount of withdrawal and inclusion into the classroom situation will naturally depend upon the needs and abilities of the individual, the needs of the remainder of the class and, to some extent, in the early days at least, the degree of self-confidence of the class teacher in her ability to cope. Since each child will have his own full-time classroom assistant and frequent (probably daily) visits from a specialist teacher, this last consideration should not be a serious problem.

Whilst the specialist teacher will remain the responsibility of and be directly accountable to the specialist headteacher, she will of course be expected to comply with the policies and day-to-day expectations of the mainstream school and its headteacher while she is on the premises, just like any other visiting support professional. Her role is therefore to prepare and monitor programmes of work and to ensure that the child's special educational needs are being adequately met. She is not there to dictate terms, give orders or regard other staff as accountable to her. Those responsibilities are quite definitely the province of the receiving mainstream school's headteacher.

THE ROLE OF THE SPECIALIST HEADTEACHER

Under the revised system, the specialist headteacher will become head of special needs support services. The scheme will not in itself precipitate mass redundancies, since the whole idea is to encompass and extend the practical assets of a special school—that is, the experience and expertise of its staff—and to do away with the cumbersome liabilities of day-to-day administration and the restriction of the building. Our aim is therefore to invest more in people and less in buildings. The headteacher, like other special school staff, will of course need to change emphasis. This will mean spending more time and effort giving direct educational support and advice to the teaching staff and less on administrative work such as ordering equipment, completing absence returns and checking on registers—music to the ears of most heads, I would think; their energies can at last be concentrated on doing the job they were trained to do and are best at.

Our present educational system seems to reward people more, the farther they distance themselves from children and the sharp end of the business. Headteachers especially seem to be constantly attending meetings, few of which bear any fruit and which generally serve to leave the head in one purposeless turmoil after another. Frustration seems abundant and job satisfaction remote. Staff constantly complain that they never see their head and yet the head seems to be putting in hour after hour and never reducing the tower of self-perpetuating paper-work. The printed directives received almost daily from the Department of Education and Science, on the National Curriculum alone, are surely enough to account for the destruction of at least one rain forest and thereby make a significant contribution to the greenhouse effect! There are too many schools where the headteacher could go sick for the day and the majority of staff would not notice. On the other hand, if a classroom assistant in a special school is absent, the head will be on the telephone for a replacement within the hour. Sadly, our current system seems to make it easier for headteachers to attend conferences than it does for a child who has special needs to get essential equipment.

This new system, then, will allow specialist headteachers to put aside vast amounts of paperwork in favour of a direct educational input. The teaching staff of their former special school will now be peripatetic and will require regular consultations to carry out their new role effectively. They will need constant advice on situations that occur through integration, they will need support in ensuring that their children receive full benefit from the National Curriculum, and they will still need to work on their own professional development by participating, with mainstream teachers, in in-service training programmes devised by the specialist head.

The specialist headteacher will also need to satisfy himself that a child's special educational needs are being properly met. He should attend each child's annual educational review and should make himself available to parents who wish to discuss their child's progress; he should also be on hand to talk to other headteachers of the receiving mainstream schools. Furthermore, he will have an all-important role in placing children whose needs have been newly identified within the special needs support service.

The child's non-educational needs will also be a concern of the specialist headteacher who should ensure not only that supported children receive a broad and balanced curriculum, but that physiotherapists, occupational therapists, speech therapists, teachers for visually impaired children, teachers for hearing impaired children, educational psychologists, clinical psychologists, and anyone else who has a role to play, remain in touch and give regular support to the children and their families.

THE ROLE OF THE CLASS TEACHER IN THE RECEIVING MAINSTREAM SCHOOL

The duty of the class teacher is to incorporate her new pupil with the minimum of fuss, in the same way that she would any other newly acquired child. Usually it is completely unnecessary for her to have preliminary chats with her class beforehand, unless of course the pupil in question has a particular need that is life-threatening. Otherwise, young children soon get to grips with their new class member by simply asking questions about them as the interest and need arises. 'Why can't he talk?' 'Will she ever be able to walk?' 'Was he born like that?' 'Does it hurt her to have that?' The questions will doubtless be myriad and they all deserve an immediate and honest straightforward answer. It is answers to these questions that develop the class's ownership of these special needs. In my experience to date, care, support, concern and acceptance by the other children have always been forthcoming. The only problems that have been encountered have come entirely from adults.

Working with another adult in the class can sometimes take a bit of getting used to and, where possible, it is always a good idea for the classroom assistant to take up her post a week or so before the supported child is introduced. This provides an excellent opportunity for the classroom assistant to get to know the other children, the layout and routines of the class, and to become acquainted with the teacher. It will be up to the class teacher to make her assistant feel at home, just as she will the child. Although they will be working on their own initiative for much of the time, classroom assistants will need a fair amount of direction from the class teacher in the early days, to discover exactly what is expected of them. Class teachers have the same responsibility towards the child who has special needs as they do for any other child in the class. However, they do have a lot of assistance available to enable them to cope with this responsibility and they should never hesitate to consult the classroom assistant, specialist teacher, physiotherapist, speech therapist, educational psychologist, parents, or anyone else who can help them give the best educational service they possibly can.

THE ROLE OF THE HEADTEACHER OF THE RECEIVING MAINSTREAM SCHOOL

The headteacher is responsible for all the pupils in his school, whether they have special needs or not, and it will be up to him to ensure that the supported pupil, is having his other special educational needs adequately met. He can do this with the help and advice of the head of support services, who will endeavour to see that every assistance is given, by way of resources, personnel and equipment, and non-educational services. Between them, these two heads will monitor the child's progress and be accountable to both the parents and the Local Education Authority. They will also decide where in the school the child should be placed. Wherever possible, this should be done on the basis of chronological age, irrespective of the child's degree of special needs. If supported children are to move on into the mainstream secondary school at the age of eleven, it is important that they do so with the support and insight that will have developed from the bond they undoubtedly form with the rest of their class during the primary years. Heads will also need to take the initiative at the child's annual educational review and see to it that these are conducted in a positive and effective way.

This alternative system of special education can work to everyone's advantage. From the child's point of view, he or she will be able to experience normality on a daily basis, included in and benefiting from good models of learning. He will also be in a better position to develop real friendships with other children who live nearby and so will be more likely to enrich his leisure time both after school and at weekends. As for his classmates, at the very least they will learn that such children exist and live in their own neighbourhood; but they will also have normality brought into their lives as they begin to acknowledge that our world is made up of a whole range of people, all of whom have a right to equal opportunity and equal value.

In the same way, parents will be able to share an understanding, and those who have a child with learning difficulties will become less isolated from their local community. Parents will also have greater choice in regard of the education that their sons and daughters receive.

As for staff, they will have a far more flexible way to deliver their service. It will enable them to meet the special educational needs of the children in their care in a more direct way, and will give them a chance to devise a more individual and personalised programme for each supported child.

Finally, the Local Educational Authority will be better off, too. It will no longer need to spend considerable sums on what are essentially non-educational resources. Since its investment will be in people rather than buildings, its assets will be more mobile and it will be better placed to supply demand wherever and whenever it is needed. Generally speaking, its assets will remain assets and not become liabilities, since people, unlike buildings, do not on the whole need to have roofs repaired, central heating replaced and woodwork regularly painted.

This rationale seemed to make perfect sense to a small number of us in Stockport. The formula seemed simple enough; all that was needed was for someone to put it into practice.

Part Two

IMPLEMENTING THE CHANGE

5 The Overdale Experience

About four or five years ago, Stockport Education Authority took the decision to reorganise its provision for special education. As a result, those special schools which had previously accommodated children of all ages were each divided into two schools, one catering for nursery and primary-aged children and the other for secondary-aged students. Whilst this might be regarded as something of a missed opportunity to make changes that would revolutionise the delivery of special educational services in the area, it did at least show that the Education Committee understood that spending up to seventeen years in the same building was perhaps of little advantage to the children within. After all, if the children had been the Great Train Robbers, with good behaviour they would have been released long before that! Too many Authorities continue to this day to operate on an all-aged basis. In some areas, a child who has severe learning difficulties will enter his nursery class at the age of two years, or sometimes even younger; then at five years of age he will be placed in the infant class of the same school. When he is seven years old he will enter the junior class and he will stay there until he reaches the age of eleven, when he will be moved into secondary education, still in the same school. At sixteen he will enter the school's further education department and finally, at the age of nineteen, he will cross the playground to take up his place in an adult training centre. Consequently he will spend his whole life within an area of a few square yards, segregated from everyone else in the community.

My task when I came to Stockport was to take up the post of

headteacher at Overdale School. This was a brand new special school—or rather an empty infant school that had been converted into a special school. It was, however, a distinct improvement on other special schools in which I had taught, these being purpose-built establishments, although for what purpose we had never quite discovered. Overdale was intended to cater for children from the age of two to eleven years, who were identified as having a severe learning difficulty. Right from the start, my staff and myself felt it was essential to ascertain precisely what it was we were trying to achieve. We took great care to avoid making empty statements about our aims and to do our best not to use the whiskery old educational clichés that schools can so easily slide into. Assuring ourselves that the children placed in our school would 'achieve their full potential' meant very little, when you actually got down to it. After all, who of us has ever achieved his or her full potential? I sincerely hope I haven't. Imagine how boring it would be if we did. What would we do then? That, I suppose, must be the fly in the ointment of paradise or Shangri-la.

No, as the newly appointed staff of a newly formed special school, we did not want simply to copy the thin jargon of other schools, nor to stand with our feet placed firmly in the clouds, when it came to stating what it was that we wanted to accomplish. After all, we were going to have forty or more children, all between the ages of two and eleven years and all of whom would have severe learning difficulties. They would be in our trust for twenty-five hours each week and thirty-nine weeks each year. We needed to be clear what we would be doing with them and why.

After a good deal of debate, our aims turned out, not so surprisingly, to be much the same as those of any mainstream school. Like them, we had the responsibility, as teachers, to enrich the total experience of each young person who attended our school by providing them with opportunities which would encourage the development of their personal growth and acquisition of life skills. If this was the case, why did we need Overdale School at all? We stopped for a minute to think, then we thought again. Nobody seemed able to provide a logical answer.

'Perhaps children who have special needs would be pushed around and bullied if they attended their local school?' someone ventured. But our experience with special schools told us that more pushing around, attention-seeking and challenging behaviour went on there than anywhere else.

'Wouldn't other children be frightened or upset by those who have epilepsy?' was another concern expressed. We pondered upon it for a while and concluded that children who had special needs were children too, and as such, they never seemed to show great anxiety when any of their classmates had fits, it was just accepted as an everyday occurrence. If children who had difficulty with learning could quickly learn this, then, surely, so could others. Besides, plenty of children who have epilepsy without learning difficulties attend their mainstream school and no great fuss seems to be made of this. The questions continued and the answers continued to follow. Theoretically, at least, there appeared to be no reason whatsoever why all children should not learn together. Any child will learn, providing we as adults do not stop them from doing so.

The theory soon became practice when, a few weeks after our school opened, we asked parents of local children if they would like their sons and daughters to attend a playgroup sited within Overdale. The response was overwhelming and, within a very short space of time, a group of thirty or so non-disabled children were sharing a classroom with eight children who had severe and some of them quite profound learning difficulties. Our school immediately took on a different atmosphere: it came alive. A hubbub of children's chatter was heard, the noise of little feet scurrying here and there and the movement of tiny bodies was everywhere. The reaction of the local children towards those who had special needs was wholly unremarkable. To them, disability was invisible.

A small charge was made to the neighbourhood children for each session they attended. This enabled us to organise ourselves in the same way as any other private playgroup. With this income, not only were we able to afford staffing, but it also meant that we could purchase equipment, become members of the Pre-school Playgroups Association, take out insurances, go on field trips and still have money left over. Whilst the playgroup operated independently from a financial point of view, both the children and the staff worked as one class. If anyone had been worried about the attitude of the local parents, all fears were now dispelled. Mothers were not only paying for the privilege of sending their children to our school, but some who lived outside our area were telephoning to ask if their child could attend our 'integrated' class in preference to their own local mainstream facility.

Our playgroup went from strength to strength and everyone seemed delighted with the arrangement. Delighted, that is, until the time came when the children approached school age. Rising fives were full of excitement, and a little apprehensive too, when they began to understand that they would all be going to 'big school' soon. But not all did go to 'big school'; those who had special needs had to remain and watch their friends walk out of Overdale into the primary school across the road. They were not allowed to follow. Instead, there was no option but to place them in a class entirely composed of severely disabled children. It was back to square one for them. To all intents and purposes, this was to be the start of a life apart. Some parents were devastated as they watched normality being taken from their children's lives and replaced by 'special' things. Their children were not yet five years old.

Our special school had only been open for a few weeks and yet it was already clear to some of us that it had to close if we were to give 'special' children the one thing they really needed: an ordinary life. Without doubt, this was not going to be easy. Local councillors get their names engraved on plaques for erecting special schools, not for taking them away. If anything, this was going to lose rather than gain them votes. If we were to change our service so radically, there would have to be a good deal of discussion with the consumers of our service. As in any other school, these we saw as being the parents.

The first thing we did was commit our thoughts to paper. This we then circulated to all parents and embarked upon a series of group meetings. These meetings became quite heated at times, to say the least, and emotions ran high. As a new school, one of our first priorities was to let parents know what to expect. We had to impress on them that they were not just welcome, but could have real influence over the shape their school was to take. A school, after all, is not merely the bricks and mortar, but a collective term given to the people who make it up—children, staff and parents. We wanted to ensure that parents, as consumers, were given every opportunity to let us know exactly how they felt about a wide range of issues.

THE PARENTS' CHARTER

Our school's policy in respect to parents was to encourage a true partnership which we hoped would result in the best possible provision being made for their children. Having first visited every parent, each in their own home, a Parents' Charter was written which outlined a list of ten guarantees. With the approval of our governing body, it was distributed to everyone whose child attended Overdale School.

PARENTS' CHARTER

1   **No information or written document held in our school, concerning a child, will be kept confidential from the child's parents.**

Whilst this seemed to worry some members of staff, nobody could give a clear indication why this should not happen.

'But this would mean that any parent could look at a child's school file at any time,' someone said with a look of alarm on her face.

'Yes?' was the rather dour reply, implying 'whyever not?'

'Well, what about confidential medical information?' The word 'medical' was lingered over as though it were somehow sacred.

We asked our school's medical officer whether she held confidential information about the children who attended our school and she confirmed that she probably did. We asked what could be so secret about the child that even their parents could not be told. After some pondering, nothing came to mind. The anxious member of staff continued unconvinced.

'But what if the parents themselves, without realising it, were major contributors to their child's developmental delay?'

'So how does it help to write it down secretly and file it away?' said a voice from the corner. 'Surely someone would have to discuss it with them at some time.'

The matter was settled, and we wrote to all other agencies to inform them of our policy and to tell them that, in future, all written information sent by them to our school would be made accessible to parents.

---

2   Parents are entitled to visit our school and be welcomed into it at any time.

Some staff wondered if they would be quite hampered on occasions by parents invading the classroom and stopping them from teaching. In practice, this never happened, and in fact the effect on teaching standards of parents on the premises was similar to a visit from Her Majesty's Inspectorate.

3 Our school will take every opportunity to consult with parents on all matters concerning their child's needs.

This was a comprehensive statement which included everything from permanently moving members of staff from one part of our school to another, to inviting parents to interview candidates for all our vacancies, including that of deputy head teacher.

4 Parents will have direct access to information concerning our school's curriculum and programmes of work designed for their child. They will also be made aware of all services and resources which can be made available to them, from both within and outside our school.

For those who wanted, we involved all parents in the development of our school's curriculum. Each teacher was allocated responsibility for a core area of the curriculum and held weekly group discussions with parents and other professional disciplines to create a written curriculum document.

All parents were also asked to participate in identifying their child's special needs and in devising specific programmes of work. As far as support services were concerned, we kept parents informed by compiling our own directory of both statutory and voluntary organisations which operated in the locality. This was quite useful, but needed to be maintained and updated at regular intervals.

5   **Parents will be entitled and encouraged to take part in all or any of our school's In-service training programmes.**

Parents not only participated in these In-service days, but eventually also gave talks themselves and organised some very relevant and interesting discussion groups.

6   **Whilst parents will be welcomed into any part of our school, they will also have a room that will be designated for their exclusive use.**

As it happened, this room was rarely used, except on occasions when they held meetings exclusively for parents, so that they could have frank, uninhibited discussions about the school. Most of the time they used all parts of the school and often took their lunch with staff in the staff room. Whilst some members of staff had expressed some reservations about parents sharing their break times with them in the staff room, when it actually came down to it, they felt perfectly at home with the situation. Strange how for even the simplest thing, people can always find reasons why it should *not* be done.

7   **Teachers will visit parents in their own homes after school hours on request, to discuss their son's or daughter's progress and needs. Such visits can be arranged on a mutually convenient basis.**

This operated under the then new Government guidelines of 1,265 hours' service from teachers. All members of the teaching staff at Overdale felt they could devote at least 40 hours to home visits, outside direct child contact time.

8 At parents' request, staff will be pleased to contact them each week or more often, to relay information on how their child has performed at school. This can be done either by telephone or in the form of a regular diary.

Keeping in regular touch with parents about their child's accomplishments, anxieties and any other relevant information is particularly important where a child has difficulty in communicating. Knowing that on a certain day your son has managed to tie his own shoelaces for the first time can reduce both his frustration and yours when he comes through the door full of excitement and incoherent speech.

9 All injuries or any ill-effects suffered by their child will be reported to parents directly, as soon as possible, either in writing, or by telephone, or in person.

This is self-explanatory and a requirement of any school.

10 All parents will be entitled to elect or be nominated for election for membership of our school's governing body every four years.

This, of course, is the legal right of all parents and they should be made aware of it. Our partnership with parents at Overdale was particularly enhanced by the fact that our Chair of Governors was also the parent of a child who attended our school.

The sequence of events in our meeting parents was as shown in Figure 2. Before they even visited our school, many parents had already agreed their child's statement of special needs with

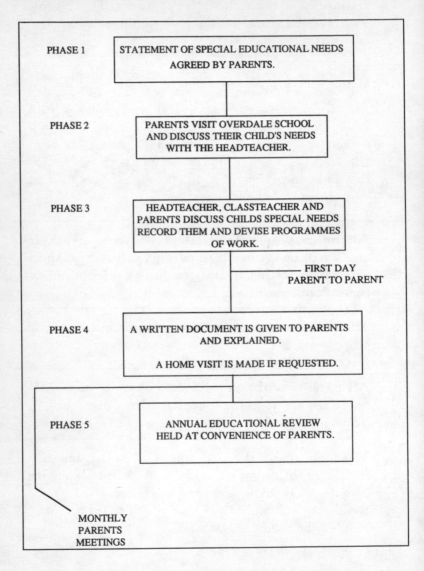

PHASE 1   STATEMENT OF SPECIAL EDUCATIONAL NEEDS
           AGREED BY PARENTS.

PHASE 2   PARENTS VISIT OVERDALE SCHOOL
           AND DISCUSS THEIR CHILD'S NEEDS
           WITH THE HEADTEACHER.

PHASE 3   HEADTEACHER, CLASSTEACHER AND
           PARENTS DISCUSS CHILDS SPECIAL NEEDS
           RECORD THEM AND DEVISE PROGRAMMES
           OF WORK.

                                    FIRST DAY
                                    PARENT TO PARENT

PHASE 4   A WRITTEN DOCUMENT IS GIVEN TO PARENTS
           AND EXPLAINED.

           A HOME VISIT IS MADE IF REQUESTED.

PHASE 5   ANNUAL EDUCATIONAL REVIEW
           HELD AT CONVENIENCE OF PARENTS.

MONTHLY
PARENTS
MEETINGS

Figure 2. Sequence of events for school admission.

the Local Education Authority, in the good faith that this was the special provision their child needed. During their visit to Overdale (Figure 2: Phase 2) they would be given a copy of our school's curriculum and a copy of the Parents' Charter. Overdale's school building had been recently adapted, so it was bright and pleasant. It was also situated in a delightful residential area. Nevertheless, once parents were shown into the classroom proposed for their child and were faced with disability *en masse* for the very first time, naturally enough, once they were allowed to do so they began to question whether the school really was an appropriate place for their child. Doubtless, at a time like this many parents would focus their attention upon the least able child, and wonder if that was what the future held for their own son or daughter.

Significantly, the first question a mother tends to ask when she gives birth to her baby is not, 'Is it a boy or a girl?' but rather, 'Is everything all right?' For the majority of mothers, of course, the reply can be reassuring, but for a small number a devastating and traumatic shock is in store, one which will first bring a feeling of complete numbness and later intense emotional pressure, eventually changing bit by bit the family's way of life. This happens not so much because of the child's disability—most parents can cope with that quite well—but more because of the type of services that are presented and the attitudes of others towards them. Many parents are still reeling from this shock when they are faced with the prospect of special education for their child. The secret hope that their child may 'grow out of it', or that the professionals have somehow 'got it wrong', is dissolved in one fell swoop when it is finally made official. In visual terms, it seems as if the large hairy arm of the Local Education Authority has taken hold of their child and, in indelible ink, stamped the words 'severe learning difficulties' across him. The next moment they are confronted with a roomful of children, all of whom have serious disablements, and told, 'This is where your child should go to school.'

At times like this, parents needed to know in what other

ways their child's needs could be met, but in official terms they were really given no other alternative. As far as the education system was concerned, the procedure was clear. These parents had a child who was under eleven years of age. That child had been formally statemented and given the label 'severe learning difficulties', therefore the only school designated to cater for him would be Overdale School. As headteacher, my discussion with parents (Figure 2: Phase 2) always began by trying to discover what they thought the needs of their child were. More often than not these turned out to bear little resemblance to what had already been written in Section Two of their Statement. As far as most parents were concerned, they simply wanted to be able to do the everyday things like other families. They wanted to be able to let their son play outside with the other children, without the fear of him being knocked down by a car. They wanted to be able to take their daughter shopping in the local supermarket, without her continually pushing over stacked cans and interfering with the other customers. It was difficulties like these which led to their child's life becoming restricted and their own life as a family becoming more and more confined and uncertain.

At this stage some parents would decide to appeal against their child's statement of special needs, or at least seek further consultation with education officers against their child's placement within a special school like Overdale. Others, whilst they were very concerned about their son or daughter attending a special school, did not feel they had the confidence, resources, stamina or ability to bring about a significant change in their child's statement of special needs. There were also some parents, although by comparison very few in number, who accepted a placement for their infant in Overdale because they could not visualise him coping in a mainstream school. Most parents, however, recognised that they needed, or would need at some time in the future, information about the support that would be available to them locally, from both the voluntary and statutory sectors. We therefore gave them a copy of our local directory as a reference.

Those parents who, for one reason or another, chose to accept a place for their youngster at Overdale, were then invited to discuss their child's needs with the class teacher and the headteacher (Figure 2: Phase 3), and to co-operate in devising specific programmes of work. This sometimes took place before their child started school, but more often afterwards, to give the class teacher a chance to get to know her new pupil. The first day at school, with all its strangeness and uncertainty will create a certain amount of stress and anxiety for any child and his parents. To make this a little easier, we operated a parent-to-parent scheme, which meant that another parent would see to it that she was on hand to make the newcomers feel welcome and to answer any questions relating to our school's day-to-day routines. Parents could identify with one another very easily and were in a good position to allay anxieties. A week or two later, a written document (Figure 2: Phase 4) containing details of the agreed programmes of work would be sent to parents and, if requested, a visit to their home would be made by the class teacher. In the meantime, all parents would be invited to meet regularly on a monthly basis, to have coffee and to discuss issues of mutual interest. These meetings were usually very well attended.

The final part in the cycle (Figure 2: Phase 5) was the annual educational review, when we examined what progress the child had made, discussed whether there was any significant change in his needs and made sure that parents were satisfied with our service. Having experienced the nature of segregated education for their child, compared this with what went on in our integrated class in Overdale and had an opportunity to talk over educational issues with other parents at the monthly meetings, many parents now began to want to do something about seeking a placement for their child in the local mainstream school, even though they might have been reluctant, for one reason or another, to do so initially.

EMPOWERING PARENTS

If parents are to get the services they want for their children, rather than the services that professionals think they need, then the balance of power that exists between service users and service providers must be redressed. Currently, as far as the provision of human services is concerned, it is unmistakably the professionals who hold all the trump cards. They control the budgets, both capital and revenue. They design and build the services. They employ the personnel to staff these services and dictate their salaries, terms of contract, qualifications, job description and hours of work. They monitor and define the quality assurance of the service and they decide who can use the service, when, where and how. In this way, inefficient and poorly delivered services can thrive whilst those whom they are intended to support can go to the wall.

It is quite different when it comes to using the everyday services in the high street. Whether it be dry cleaning, video hire or a haircut, in the real world the growth of commercial services and the standards they maintain are entirely determined by whether we continue to use them or not. Here, we have a considerably wider choice; each of us monitors our own level of quality assurance and the service provider is fully aware of the importance of meeting the service users' requirements. Indeed, the customer is always right. In contrast, when it comes to providing services to meet the needs of people who are elderly, those who have a learning difficulty or any other state service designed to meet human needs, the system seems to work in reverse.

The difference is, of course, that in the commercial sector the consumer has control of the economy because he has purchasing power, whereas in state-provided services he has no power at all. It is rather like saying that you will be taking 20 per cent of each person's income away every month and spending it on what *you* think he or she should have. This year, for instance, you may decide that everybody should have a stereo music system and that it should be a black one. In the same way, human services too often try to meet individual and personal needs dictatorially and on a large-group basis. Perhaps the recent Griffiths Report will enable some changes to be made in this respect, at least as far as District Health and Social Services Departments are concerned, but that still remains to be seen. In the meantime, at Overdale School, we set about enabling parents to have greater influence over our own particular service, as far as we could. We did this by targeting certain areas in which to invite their involvement:

a) By encouraging parents to form small *ad hoc* groups from time to time. These groups would visit a range of services, including our own school, then write their own short appraisal of that service, so that they could discuss it with the staff of that service.

b) By ensuring that parents were given direct and indirect representation on all interview panels for the employment of every member of staff.

c) By encouraging parents to organise workshops and conferences for the training of staff.

d) By encouraging parents to write regular articles for professional journals and local newspapers.

e) By encouraging parents to make known the type of services they sought for the future.

To begin with, parents were more than a little unsure of themselves. They were not at all unsure of the services they were seeking, I hasten to say, but somewhat apprehensive about tasks like writing articles, interviewing staff and giving presentations. Activities like these did not come easily to most people at first, and they had to learn to apply themselves to them. Many of them were women who had for some years been confined mostly to domestic chores and had had their time committed to bringing up their children. They needed to refresh themselves in certain skills and to summon up a little self-confidence. Some took up adult classes in creative writing during the daytime, while their children were at school.

Others involved themselves by going to various conferences, and two became school governors, one of whom was and still is the Chairperson.

As time went on, their confidence grew rapidly. Those who were more articulate gave their support to those who were less so, and eventually the parents formed a properly constituted group to give themselves both the credibility that comes with an organised structure and total independence. This group they called Passport, and it continues to exist today. It aims to help parents anywhere, who wish to gain a place for their son or daughter in their local mainstream school, with support, irrespective of the child's degree of disability.

OUR PILOT STUDY

Whilst parents were endeavouring to find better and more varied ways of voicing their thoughts, and whilst the advantages of an inclusive education were becoming more apparent through the establishment of our private playgroup, it fell upon me as headteacher to approach the Education Authority in order to propose what in effect would mean the closure of our own special school—a school which the Education Committee had opened only a few weeks previously. I was going to have to face more than just the raising of a few eyebrows.

In a letter outlining our suggestions, I explained to the education officers that in line with Central Government legislation and the national trend, Stockport Education Authority had for some time now held a declared policy of commitment to the integration of children who have special needs into mainstream educational provision. I also pointed out that already, since the 1981 Education Act, they had successfully incorporated a number of such children into primary and secondary schools throughout the borough. These, however, were mostly children who had a hearing or visual impairment or some sort of physical disability. Therefore, in pursuance of their policy on integration, I enclosed a document which described a suggested operational strategy for implementing

Stockport's policy in relation to those pupils, up to the age of eleven years, who had severe learning difficulties (that is, those who were currently in attendance at Overdale School).

Shortly after sending this letter, I was invited to the Education Divisional Offices and a discussion took place. Despite the newness of our school and the considerable financial commitment that Stockport Education Authority had recently contributed to it, the committee eventually agreed that a pilot study should be made of our proposals, in order to assess their merit and feasibility. A small working party was formed, consisting of a parent, an educational psychologist, a headteacher of a mainstream school, an education officer, a school governor and myself. This expanded later to include others. Initially, it was the responsibility of this working party to:

1 State the aims of the pilot study.
2 Declare the criteria to be used for the selection of those children who would be participating.
3 Declare the criteria to be used for the selection of participating staff.
4 Decide how the pilot study was to be evaluated and by whom.
5 Project what the cost and resource implications of the pilot study would be.
6 Draft a job description for the supporting classroom assistants.
7 Declare the accountability of staff.
8 Devise a record-keeping system which would keep an account of each child's progress and programmes of work.
9 Explore the possibility of alternative funding.
10 Create opportunities for participating families and staff to meet each other regularly.

As a result, the working party decided to offer *five* families whose children had severe learning difficulties the opportunity of full-time places for their sons and daughters within their local nursery, infant or primary school, whichever they would have attended had they not been previously identified as having special needs. Their placement in school would therefore be made purely on the basis of their place of residence and their chronological age. Each child would be provided with a full-time classroom assistant who would work under the supervision of the class teacher, together with the guidance and advice of a visiting specialist teacher. This specialist teacher was to be made available on a full-time basis, from Overdale School, exclusively for the selected five children. The specialist teacher would be able to allocate her time so that she could spend a full day each week with each child, or an hour every day per child. The period of evaluation was to be for one full academic year and a written report of the findings was to be presented to the Director of Education, parents, school governors, staff and other interested parties. An evaluation of the proceedings was to be carried out by two educational psychologists within the Education Authority and, independently, by psychologists from the Hester Adrian Research Centre at Manchester University.

THE AIMS OF OUR PILOT STUDY

The aims of our pilot study were many and varied. Not all of them would be easily measurable and we recognised, too, that with a small sample of just five children, much of the evaluation would need to be descriptive. According to the 1981 Education Act, all children should have the opportunity to attend their local mainstream school, unless they suffer by being placed there, cause other pupils to suffer by their presence there or if their placement in the mainstream school is not an efficient use of the Local Authority's resources. The Act makes no mention whatsoever of the misguided view held by some people, that the placed children should academically improve. Indeed, it does not require them to show any form of progress at all while they are there. Maintaining their supported place in mainstream education therefore need not be dependent upon their achieving any particular educational goals. Children who have declared special needs are meant to attend their local mainstream school first and foremost, simply to be included. Our pilot study was to determine whether, during this process, children who have severe learning difficulties would have a better chance of their needs being met if they were supported by special staff and resources within the mainstream setting rather than in a segregated special school. We were also to establish that the process of inclusion for our selected children would, at the very least, not disadvantage them educationally, medically or socially.

In particular, we set out to achieve the following objectives:

a)   To determine the level of support necessary in order to carry out this alternative system of special education effectively.

b)   To increase the learning opportunities of the included child.

c)   To achieve a satisfactory level of social and functional integration.

d)   To increase the skills and confidence of the staff in mainstream schools, when coping with the severe learning difficulties of children included in their class.

e)   To change negative attitudes, where they exist, and increase the degree of liberal acceptance amongst staff and pupils within mainstream establishments, of children who have severe learning difficulties.

f)   To provide information on which to base policy decisions on the future of special education in Stockport Metropolitan Borough Council.

Our stated operational parameters for this pilot study were:

1   That participation should be open to all children who currently attended Overdale School, and should be subject only to parent self-selection.

2   Any child participating in the pilot study should not in any
    way be disadvantaged in terms of curriculum oppor-
    tunities or access to support services such as physiotherapy
    or speech therapy, in comparison with those that presently
    existed at Overdale School.
3   Neither children who have special needs nor the children
    who have no such special needs should be disadvantaged as
    a result of the pilot study.

THE SEQUENCE OF EVENTS LEADING TO OUR PILOT STUDY

In September 1987 Overdale School opened.

October 1987   Parents of Overdale School were given a
                    written outline of the proposed pilot
                    study, having discussed the issues of inclu-
                    sive education quite extensively for two
                    months. This written outline was to be-
                    come our document for formal discussion
                    and it gave an overview of the general
                    philosophy with an explanation of our
                    proposed study and its specific aims.

November 1987   The Governors of Overdale School, who
                    had received a copy of the same written
                    document as the parents, had discussed its
                    contents formally and offered their unan-
                    imous support.

November 1987   Parents met yet again to discuss the written
                    proposals of our pilot study.

November 1987   As headteacher, I met parents individually
                    to talk about the likely implications of the
                    pilot study for their own children.

January 1988   The closing date was given as a last oppor-
                    tunity for parents to put forward their

child's name for selection as one of the five children who would be required for our pilot study.

January 1988   The actual selection took place of the five children who were to participate in the pilot study. This was done by random 'lottery'.

Somehow, the notion of choosing our participating children by simply drawing their names from a hat did not seem to be a proper and appropriately dignified method of selection. Nevertheless, none of us could think of a better way of ensuring the infallible fairness that it seemed to guarantee. The idea of our pilot study was to test our philosophy, which was that *any* child could be successfully included in his or her local school community, whatever the severity of disablement or degree of special need. With this in mind, we certainly did not want to choose children for our pilot study other than in a purely random way. We decided that names should be picked from a hat in the presence of the full working party. We also stipulated that the names of the selected children would not be made known until the headteacher of each local school had agreed to take the child and to participate in our pilot project. This was done just in case one of the receiving headteachers refused to accept our child within his school, which might well be upsetting for the parents if they knew. We therefore agreed beforehand with parents that the selected names would not be announced until their local mainstream school had said that they would co-operate. This also meant that headteachers of the receiving mainstream schools would not feel under pressure to accept a child simply because the parents might know if they refused. With the parents' agreement, then, we established a selection procedure which allowed us to approach their child's local mainstream school and, if they were not in favour, the next nearest school; then, if the child was still rejected, his name would be discarded and a new name chosen from the 'infamous' hat. As it happened, there was no need for us to discard any of the chosen names as they were all accepted, four by their local school and one by the school in the next catchment area.

January 1988   Adverts were to be placed in the local news-
paper for applications for the five classroom
assistant posts. Job descriptions were also to be
drafted.

In drafting this advertisement, we made it clear to all potential candidates that no formal qualifications were required. We simply wanted to employ people who were interested in working with children, could learn quickly, work well in a team, be flexible and had a good sense of humour. For the five posts we received one hundred and twenty completed applica-tion forms. Some were from qualified nurses, qualified teachers, nursery nurses, and physiotherapists, whilst others had no formal qualifications at all. We tried to determine those applications who showed promise, not by professional or academic certificates, but by the way in which their letter of application had been written. From the one hundred and twenty applications we short-listed twenty (rather a lottery in itself, I'm afraid, as so many short-listings of this kind tend to be) and asked them to attend a first interview. From these we chose eight candidates who attended a final interview a week later, and of these we engaged the five staff we needed, keeping names and addresses of the others who were inter-ested in carrying out future supply work.

January 1988   Accompanied by the deputy head of Overdale
School, I visited the five local mainstream
placements of the selected children, in order to
introduce the nature of our pilot study to the
headteachers and to ask for their agreement to
participate.

The thought of coping with the special needs of a child who had severe learning difficulties naturally made most head-teachers extremely cautious. Some of them pointed out that they already had a number of children in their school who had been statemented for one reason or another, but they had only been given extra staffing for just a few hours each week to accommodate all these children's special needs. Nearly all headteachers were suspicious, fearing that the Local Education Authority would take advantage of them. In the past they had often been asked to place children who had special needs, but had been given very little, if any staff, resources, support or advice with which to meet these needs. Moreover, what little extra staffing had been provided by the Education Authority initially was often whittled away shortly afterwards.

This gap of mistrust between the Local Education Office and headteachers appears to be quite universal. The mistrust also works both ways, in that education officers who are responsible for controlling budgets often feel, and are some-times justified in their suspicions, that some headteachers continue to declare a need for additional support staff when a child's special needs have become far less prominent and no longer warrant it. Some headteachers also felt that access to their school might well be a problem. Space and access throughout their school building was sometimes held at rather a premium. Whilst there was some cause for them to be concerned about this, often these excuses were just symptoms of their anxieties about coping. After all, how much space does one need in a school to accommodate one extra child? Problems of space or accessibility often turned out to be problems of attitude more than anything else.

In one primary school, where they had included a seven-year-old girl who was confined to a wheelchair for most of the day, they had encountered some problems at times in getting her from A to B. Over a period of weeks a variety of workmen, engineers and council officials, fully equipped with clipboards, slide rules and forms to sign in triplicate, had come and gone, measured and stroked their chins thoughtfully while they considered the difficulty. In the meantime, a class of seven-year-olds had measured and sawn wood in their craft, design and technology lessons, producing a series of very effective hand-made ramps, because they had noticed that their classmate was experiencing difficulty in getting into some parts of the school. The expensive estimate that followed the numerous visits of the adults, of course, became quite unnecessary.

In most places, access is usually fairly easily and inexpensively overcome if people only have a positive attitude. That is not to say that there will be some buildings which present real difficulties, but these tend to be few and far between. One has to ask how they cope in such schools with parents who are disabled and want to attend their child's open day, or teachers who have a mobility problem and have applied for a teaching post in the school. One headteacher expressed concern about his school's lack of proper toilet facilities for a child with disabilities, unaware that he was actually standing in front of a door bearing a sign in large red letters proclaiming it to be a toilet for disabled users. When this door was opened, the spacious toilet area was full of supplies stored there by the caretaker. It is strange how headteachers often seem to have these anxieties about toileting, as though people who are disabled somehow have a curiously different digestive system from the rest of us.

A number of headteachers stipulated that they wanted to visit the child while he or she was still at Overdale School, before they agreed to accept him in their own school. This we vigorously resisted whenever possible, as we felt that the notion of heads 'viewing' the child within a special school environment not only resembled a cattle market, but also meant that they would probably be looking more at the child's degree of disability than at the child himself. We much preferred to arrange a short accompanied visit to the mainstream school by the child, where he or she could be seen by heads and staff as a child like any other, but with the additional attribute of special needs. This way people seemed to respond far more appropriately, focusing on the child rather than on the nature of his or her disability.

In the past I had noticed exactly the same reaction from sixth form students who had carried out work experience in special schools. Many of these students had arrived on our campus rather sheepishly, not knowing quite what to expect. As the products of a segregated education system, they seemed to have acquired a fear of the unknown. This was very different from our experience with the local pre-school children, who showed no such fear or reluctance to share a classroom with other children who happened to be disabled. In fact, for many, it appeared that disability went quite unnoticed. When it was noticed, there was some curiosity and a wish to be supportive, but never any fear. As far as the sixth-formers were concerned, their attitudes never failed to change completely by the end of their first day. Their mood changed rapidly, too, from one of nervous uncertainty to a deluge of enthusiasm. Far from being reluctant to enter our school, it often seemed that they could hardly wait to return to the children again the next day. It was as though they were somehow relieved to discover that children who attend special schools turn out to be just children after all, not the strangely concocted product of science fiction that their segregated experience had allowed them to conjure up in their imagination.

January 1988　Parents visited their child's proposed main-　　　　　　　stream school placement.

Once each of the selected schools had been approached and the headteacher had agreed to participate, the parents visited their child's placement so that they, too, could give their approval. All parents did so quite readily. Some of them had actually been to the school themselves as children. Some parents, I suspect, particularly those whose children had more profound learning difficulties, secretly wondered just how it would all work out in practice and how they would feel if their child did not manage to fit in as well as they hoped. The arrangement for all the children participating in our pilot study was that they would be removed from the integrated situation immediately and returned to Overdale School, if at any time either the parents or the headteacher thought that the child was being caused to suffer, or that the children in his class were suffering by his presence. This was naturally a stressful situation for the parents, who often felt that they were living under Damocles' suspended sword. If the worst happened, how would they cope emotionally with yet another rejection from those who made up their local community? It is always done in the nicest way of course:

'We think it would be better for you if . . .'

When you think about it, having to ask if your child can be allowed to attend his local school is just another example of the infringement of people's civil liberties, for although these children lived within the school's catchment area, just like the other children, and were the relevant age to attend the school, just like the other children, *unlike* the other children they not only had to ask if they could attend their local school but, despite the provision of a full-time classroom assistant and part-time specialist teacher to support their special needs, they had to prove continuously, on a daily basis, to the satisfaction of the headteacher, that they were worthy of staying there.

April 1988   The employment of the classroom assistants.

I think it would have been much better if we had begun our pilot study in either January or September, since these are the months when schools usually admit their new intake for the year. Our children would then have started at the same time as the rest of the children in their class. As it was, the education officers were rather governed by the financial year when it came to funding this project, so were unable to employ our five classroom assistants before April 1988.

When we did so, we made another mistake by basing them initially within Overdale School itself. The idea was that they could get to know the children they were to pair with and would have the support of specialist staff before entering their allotted mainstream schools. Looking back, however, this made very little sense, as all it really achieved was to instil in them a false association with our own special school and a false alliance with each other. What we needed them to do was to align themselves with their own mainstream school.

I think the classroom assistants actually found themselves rather isolated at this stage, in a no-man's land. The whole object of the exercise was to remove the child they were supporting from a special school and relocate him successfully within his local school. However, they seemed to fall between two evils. Whilst we dissuaded them from too much contact with Overdale School, at the same time they were not, in the beginning at least, completely included and recognised by the mainstream schools as 'proper' members of staff. After all, the whole operation was understandably rather threatening for mainstream staff and they viewed the situation as one does a new next-door neighbour, smiling politely from a distance, but not making the mistake of being over-welcoming too early. With the responsibility of thirty or more children in their class, the concept of inclusive education had to be proved to them, not the other way round. It also had to be done, we felt, without disturbing the balance of their routine day.

The classroom assistants were only too aware of this, but whilst they were anxious to maintain their new school's normal equilibrium, they did not yet know what that state of normal equilibrium was. Until relationships had been established and a certain amount of readjustment had taken place all round, I think it is true to say that the mainstream staff in general felt quite nervous about the whole venture, and that the specialist staff felt they must act as seasoned diplomats, continually treading on eggshells.

On reflection, I am sure that we would have done very much better if we had based our newly appointed classroom assistants in the homes of the children whom they were going to support, and allowed them to get to know both the child and the child's special needs in a neutral place, with the knowledge and experience of the child's parents on hand to help them. As it was, they assembled at Overdale School for the first few weeks, where they spent time working together with all the selected pilot study children in one group. Our idea was that they should get to know each other and that the matching of child and classroom assistant would happen through a natural process.

Some members of our working party felt that the classroom assistant should also undergo a form of in-service training. I rather believed, and still believe, that the real needs of a child automatically become apparent in an 'ordinary life' situation, and that indoctrinating newcomers into our own conditioned ways of thinking about the nature and remediation of severe learning difficulties only serves to deprive us of the chance of acquiring new insights, from people who are new to this field and not yet marred by narrowed thinking. In my view it was regrettable that we attempted to 'train' new people in our professionally established but dubious techniques, rather than taking this rare opportunity to expand and develop our own understanding by listening to their impressions.

Nevertheless, due to pressure from psychologists, we opted to carry out a three-day EDY (Education of the Developmentally Young) course for each of the five classroom assistants. This shared training, in my opinion, did not really help any of them to appreciate their child's individual and personal needs. In fact, at one point, soon after the classroom assistants had started work at their mainstream schools, they began to take their children out of school and meet as a group to go swimming together. It was the fact that we had first based these staff together and offered them training together that had brought about this situation which, of course was entirely contrary to our aim. We had created in the staff a need to seek support from each other rather than from the staff in their mainstream schools, the parents and the specialist teacher. Suffice to say that the children themselves did not need this 'special outing' at all, and the practice stopped almost as soon as it had started.

During April 1988 several visits were made by the supported child and his or her classroom assistant both to the child's home and to the mainstream school where they were to be placed. This continued until May 1988 when the pilot study began in earnest, full-time.

6   Children of the Pilot Study

To us they were like lunar astronauts, our five intrepid children, when they made their one small step which was to take them across that great invisible divide into their local mainstream schools, for the first time in their lives. Even now they would be under daily scrutiny and, as far as many of the adults were concerned, it would be easy for them to outstay such welcome as they had. The British in particular appear to have some sort of built-in aversion to change; it seems so much easier to look for the drawbacks, no matter how obscure they may be, than to acknowledge some of the overwhelming benefits. We wondered if our comprehensive education system would show itself to be truly comprehensive, or whether long-established, illogical fears and prejudices would prevent five small children from having access to the dubious normality that the other youngsters and their families were granted, without the indignity of having to ask.

LAUREN

Lauren was eight years old when she was selected by way of our random 'football draw' method to be given the opportunity to participate in our pilot study. She was, and still is, a pretty child with a pleasant disposition. She is profoundly disabled, which means that she is unable to walk or stand without assistance, and at that time she was also unable to speak. She often makes loud babbling noises when she is excited and, like many young children, cries when she is presented with new situations that she does not immediately

Lauren with her friends at playbreak.

like or understand. Her local primary school operates on an open-plan basis and every available space is fully used. It is a bright, stimulating environment, inviting and colourful. Corridors are teaching areas and as such often take on the guise of a cave or a rocket, or some other structure that excites children's imagination and curiosity.

During her time in a special school Lauren had acquired a good deal of bulky equipment. A standing frame, which resembled some artefact from the Spanish Inquisition, a changing bench to assist with her double incontinence, and her wheelchair were among her remarkable collection of metal frames, wooden panels and assorted screws. I was sometimes inclined to believe that it might have been simpler to hire a scaffolding company to assist Lauren to walk. Nevertheless, despite her new school's restricted space, her giant Meccano system was fully accommodated, although it did make us wonder just how much of it Lauren really needed and whether we could provide it in a more compact form. Shortly after she had begun to settle in, her physiotherapist designed a monumental standing frame for her, the proportions of which were so big that Sir Edmund Hillary would not have refused the challenge to climb. It was at least a full twelve months before Hazel, our specialist teacher, and Jenny, Lauren's classroom assistant, admitted to the headteacher that they had sneaked the apparatus into the classroom after school hours and disguised it as part of the term's topic.

The Local Education Authority had provided Lauren with a formal written statement of her special educational needs, but, like most statements produced by most Education Authorities, it actually gave very little relevant information about her needs and appeared to serve more as the official documentation which showed that the Authority had complied with the law and kept the paperwork tidy. Its effect was to ensure that Lauren was placed in a separate establishment away from other children, away from the opportunity to make friends and away from the local community in general. Her statement read as follows:

Section Two (special educational needs):
Lauren attended a school for pupils with severe learning difficulties from April 1985 until September 1987, when she tranferred to Overdale School.

She needs to continue to follow an individualised developmental programme with priority given to gross motor, communication and manipulative skills. She also needs opportunities for mixing with pupils who demonstrate good models.

Section Three (provision to meet these needs):
Lauren should attend a school for pupils with severe learning difficulties and she should follow an individualised structured developmental programme which should be devised under the direction of the headteacher in consultation with the parents.

Section Four (appropriate school or other arrangements):
Lauren should attend Overdale School for pupils with severe learning difficulties.

Section Five (additional non-educational provision):
Lauren should receive physiotherapy as determined by the Health Authority.

During her first week at the primary school Lauren, as one would expect, was quite unsettled and, by her own standards, relatively noisy. This was rather worrying for her classroom assistant, who was concerned that Lauren might be rather a distraction for the other children, particularly since the school was arranged on an open-plan basis. She felt that all eyes would be on Lauren and, as her support worker, was aware of the undertaking which had been given, even before our pilot study had started, that any of the five children could be returned at a moment's notice to Overdale School if it was felt that the project was not proving successful. This fairly trivial behaviour therefore put a good deal of stress on Lauren's classroom assistant and, indeed, on her parents, too. They were all naturally anxious that the scheme should not fail, especially in its first week. In real terms, however, Lauren's noises, had no more volume than the general sounds made by the other individuals in her classroom, who in the normal course of events would call across to their friends for a pencil, or become excited over the activity in which they were busily involved. Whilst Lauren's vocalisations may initially have sounded unfamiliar to the rest of her class, they were certainly no louder than anyone else's. The trouble is that once we start attaching labels to children, we tend to attribute every little movement they make to the fact that they have special needs. Lauren's utterances were actually noticed more by the adults than by the children who, after a series of initial enquiries like, 'Can she say any words?' and, 'Will Lauren ever be able to speak?' accepted the situation for what it was, no more and no less.

To begin with, assemblies were a little embarrassing, when Lauren registered her overexcitement by punctuating the proceedings with the occasional loud shrill. After a short while, when her surroundings had become more familiar, she settled in and the shrills ceased. It must have been quite a culture shock for her when, from day one, she was constantly surrounded by other active, mobile and talkative children. Everyone wanted to be with her at once, it seemed, wherever she was. Order was maintained by the class teacher, who very soon had to insist upon a rota system for those who wanted to sit next to her at lunch time. We were a little perturbed by this, as we did not want Lauren to become regarded as the class-room pet, along with the hamster and goldfish. Whilst we much preferred the other children to show their interest and give support rather than avoiding and isolating Lauren, by the same token we did not want her to become a novelty or a curiosity which wore off after a week or so. As it happened we need not have concerned ourselves; three years on, the situation is much the same and a strong bond has been formed between Lauren and her classmates. As for the rota system, it still has to be implemented, since her popularity has not waned.

After starting our pilot study, the change in Lauren's life and that of her family was immediate. At the age of eight years, for the first time in her life, she was suddenly invited to another child's birthday party. She has had many such invitations since and has now become quite blasé about it, but at the time it underlined the fact that attending a special school miles away from her own neighbourhood for all those years had meant, quite simply, that other children hardly knew she existed. It was a significant moment, too, for her mother when, on the Saturday morning following Lauren's first week at her new school, right through the day, countless children passing by in the street called out to her, as Mum and Lauren together toured the shops. Suddenly people were aware of her, suddenly she had friends, children who liked her and wanted to stop and pass the time of day—with Lauren, that is, not with her mother, as had always been the case previously. In the past many people had tended to ignore Lauren, talking over her head to her mother and avoiding even looking at her. Now things had changed. People stopped to talk to Lauren, with little more than a cursory glance or acknowledgement for Mum. For the first time Lauren was being seen as a person in her own right.

Physiotherapy had always seemed to play a prominant part in Lauren's existence. Wherever she was, you could be sure that a bonegrinder would not be far away. Not only that: the physiotherapists seemed to come and go with some regularity. In the few years that I have known her, Lauren has had the attention of four of them. One of the disadvantages of inclusive education, put forward by those who opposed it, was that regular therapy, whether physiotherapy, speech therapy or occupational therapy, would not be readily available for those children who needed it. This made two assumptions—first, that children were already receiving such therapy on a regular basis while they attended their special school, which often they were not, and second, that the poorly resourced paramedical services would be even more thinly stretched if they were called upon to visit children in their individual schools, which are spread right across the borough.

In practice, far from creating a problem, the alternative system of special education has improved the situation quite considerably. The establishment of a full-time classroom assistant for each child means that speech therapists, physiotherapists, and anyone else for that matter, who have something to contribute, can do so on a daily basis, by directing a programme of events for the child through the support worker. In this way, the child's progress can be monitored on a monthly or six-weekly cycle and the therapist is able to reach a larger and wider clientele.

This, after all, is what happens elsewhere in the Health Service. Doctors seem to manage to direct their medical knowledge perfectly well through nurses, without the need to change bandages or give bed baths themselves. They operate on a consultancy basis, which enables them to apply their skills to a much larger number of people. When parents return home from the hospital with a child who has just been diagnosed as having epilepsy, they are likely to have no medical qualifications and no understanding whatsoever of their child's condition. They have to listen to the advice from the hospital and act accordingly. They are not given a doctor to take home with them in case their child has a seizure; they have to make the day-to-day judgements and decisions themselves, seeking help from members of the medical profession when necessary and attending regular appointments.

Advice, therefore, from therapists, specialist teachers, and anyone who can help to meet the child's special needs, can operate very effectively through just one key person, rather than through a whole barrage of people who sometimes fall over each other trying to provide the child with what they think is needed. In this way, a range of provisions can be implemented more flexibly. Physiotherapy, speech therapy, language development, mathematical concepts—whatever you care to name—can often be integrated and delivered spontaneously with far greater effect than by nominating set times for set activities. Wednesday afternoon at two o'clock may not always be the optimum moment, nor even a convenient moment, for Lauren to undergo a series of physio exercises.

At the age of two years my own daughter Mandy was diagnosed as having diabetes. Whilst I had heard of the condition, I had no idea what it was going to mean in practice, or what effect it would have on our lives when we brought her home from the hospital. Mandy's consultant took us on one side and explained the very basics and then went on to say that over the next few weeks he was going to teach us everything he knew about diabetes and how it related to our own child. This did not mean that we were going to be like doctors, who have a range of medical knowledge about a range of medical conditions for a range of people, but it did mean that we would come to learn more than anyone else about the way diabetes affected the life of our child, and how best to manage it. As Mandy grew up, of course, this knowledge was imparted to her so that she is now herself the expert on her own diabetes. The advantage of our alternative system of special education is that classroom assistants, in conjunction with parents, can learn to operate in just this way.

Before Lauren began her placement in her local mainstream school, we seemed to spend far more time and energy discussing what could go wrong than what could go right. There was some anxiety expressed about the fact that Lauren had two brothers already attending the school. How was her presence there going to affect them? Would her disability cause them embarrassment? Would they find themselves getting into fights with other children who made unkind comments? In fact, none of these things happened. In a sense, life was much easier for Lauren's brothers, who did not have to try to explain their unseen sister's disabilities whenever the occasion arose. Lauren was now there, in their midst, so descriptions were unnecessary. As for unkind comments, these simply did not happen, since the whole school was most supportive. As with all the children who have participated in our pilot study, we have found that the notion of ridicule and cruelty where disability is concerned rests largely in the minds of adults. Young children, in our experience, do not seem to pay much attention to an individual's disablement, and when they do, their attitude is one of either caring or concern. It seems that, unlike us adults, they have not yet been conditioned by a repertoire of illogical fears and prejudices.

My son Adam, at the age of four, was watching a wrestling match on television one day. One opponent was as black as coal and the other was as white as flour. I asked him which of the wrestlers he supported and received the reply,

'The one wearing the gold boots.'

Later that day, as we were driving through London, I pointed to the front door of a house we were passing, explaining that I had lived there when I was his age. As I pointed, the door opened and out came a group of Asian people. Ten minutes on, Adam looked at me very thoughtfully and finally said,

'Dad, when you were my age, were you black?'

Prejudices like phobias, are passed on from one generation to the next. At best, they limit our experience and learning. At worst, they culminate in genocide.

At the time of writing, Lauren has been attending her local primary school for three years, which in itself shows that the principle of inclusive education has been a success. During this time she has had a number of support workers, which I think is preferable to having the same person continuously. In the latter situation, there is always a risk that the support worker's enthusiasm will wane and that Lauren's dependency on her will become further entrenched. Ideally, classroom assistants should, from time to time, replace other adults in the school, so that they can rotate, each spending some time with Lauren. As a matter of policy, it would probably have been better for us to employ all the supporting classroom assistants within our pilot study on a job-share basis, so that children like

Lauren would have had one assistant in the mornings and another in the afternoons. This would have meant that supply staff, in the event of absences, would have been more readily available; moreover, In-service training could have been carried out at regular intervals, for the morning staff in the afternoon and for the afternoon staff in the morning, without loss of contact time.

Lauren's Review
Some six months after Lauren had entered her local mainstream school, her annual educational review became due. Those present were her mother, Jenny (her classroom assistant), the headteacher of Lauren's local mainstream school, Hazel (the peripatetic specialist teacher), a physiotherapist and myself (as headteacher of Overdale School). Lauren's progress was summarised as follows:

Lauren has made steady progress in all areas of her development. Particular progress has been made in expressive language and Lauren is learning to say a variety of new sounds. It is felt that she has benefited greatly from contact and stimulation with other children in her mainstream school, whose company and attention she greatly enjoys. We have seen a marked improvement in Lauren's motivation to explore her surroundings and she will now actively reach out to explore things. Lauren's recognition of single words has increased and small but important improvement has been seen in fine and gross motor activities. Lauren has also made progress with feeding herself. She has coped well with her new situation in her local mainstream primary school and has become much more tolerant of and adaptable to new situations.

PARENT'S VIEWS
a)   Lauren's mother is extremely pleased with her daughter's placement at her local mainstream school and is most anxious for this to continue. She has

noticed Lauren attempting to do things which she has not done before.

b)   Lauren's mother expressed a wish for her daughter's statement of special needs to be amended to read that she needs to attend her local mainstream primary school.

c)   Lauren's mother said that her daughter had been sleeping soundly since she had attended her local mainstream school and that this was a great improvement.

d)   Lauren's mother was very pleased and encouraged by the warm response to her daughter from the other children. She said that they came up to Lauren and spoke to her when they were out shopping, whereas before they would not have known or acknowledged her.

SPECIALIST TEACHER'S VIEWS

Lauren thoroughly enjoys the company of other children and gets much obvious pleasure from their attention or from watching them perform tasks. She seems to have made many friends since her placement in her local mainstream primary school. The children are very eager to help her and are very interested in the things we are trying to teach Lauren. They will stop her if she is chewing her clothing and they will shout encouragement or help her to move her legs when she is doing walking practice. When Lauren is in her standing frame, children passing through will pick up toys she has dropped and give them back to her, or stop to say a few words to her. Lauren's classmates are very interested in why she is unable to walk and what they can do to help her. They want to know what happens at her physiotherapy and hydrotherapy sessions. They will sometimes sign to her in Makaton or prompt her to point to the body parts she is learning.

Lauren has a close relationship with Jenny, her classroom assistant, and she will often turn to her for reassurance or seek her out with her eyes if she is presented with something different and Jenny is not in close proximity.

Since Lauren has been placed in her local mainstream primary school she has received the friendship and attention of a wide number of children, all with good language models. She has had the benefit of a full-time classroom assistant to carry out her individually designed programmes of work on a regular daily basis. This has also meant that it has been possible for her to have regular horse-riding, swimming and hydrotherapy sessions along with the flexibility of being able to use the local community facilities whenever necessary. Because her mother now brings Lauren to school and takes her home again, along with her two brothers, this means that she no longer has to worry about having to be in two places simultaneously and now has time to receive a daily report from Lauren's classroom assistant about her activities.

Less than two years before these reports were written, Lauren had been placed in a special care unit in a special school for children who had severe learning difficulties. For a little girl who was not able to adjust readily or cope well with change, she has certainly come a long way.

Nowadays, since Lauren has attended her local primary school, she continues to improve in all areas of her development. These include her eye contact with other people, her concentration, her use of eye-pointing to indicate choices and her ability to say a variety of new sounds. A marked improvement has been noticed in her general motivation to explore her surroundings, and steady achievement in the physical area of both fine and gross motor skills. Noteworthy, too, is the fact that new or strange situations no longer seem to affect her as they used to do; she is now far more adaptable in these circumstances. More important than all these attainments, however, is that whilst Lauren is always likely to have severe learning difficulties, she has now established a network of friends and an identity within her own local community. Extracts from diaries kept by her classroom assistant and by Hazel, the specialist support teacher, illustrate typical day-to-day occurrences:

SPECIALIST TEACHER

June 1988: Took Lauren out onto the playground and left her stationary in the corner. I moved away and talked to the teacher on playground duty. Children gathered round Lauren, some gave her crisps and one little girl made a daisy chain and put it on Lauren's head.

Playground duty. Went on field, sat Lauren on grass, soon surrounded by lots of children. Older girl brought puppet and showed Lauren. Played with her puppet.

September 1988: Whilst changing Lauren's splints, a few children gathered round and wanted to help put them on her legs. They wanted to know why she had new splints.

We were invited to walk to reception class and touch one of the spiders dangling from the ceiling. Lauren got a lot of encouragement from the other children to 'come on' and received a huge cheer and clap when she touched the spider.

CLASSROOM ASSISTANT

March 1989: The attitude of the children has always been superb. At first we were inundated with questions which we answered as honestly as we could and they have always wanted to help, to play with Lauren, to push her round and to be given responsibilities associated with her. This has never wavered, not even when the newness of it all wore off. This is the same for all children from reception class to Junior 4.

Recently, I am told, the teacher had a deputation of Lauren's classmates who had learnt that she was about to be admitted to hospital for a while, in order to undergo a surgical operation on her legs.

'Is this to make Lauren's feet look like our feet,' they asked, 'or is it so that she will be able to walk better?' Before the teacher could reply, they went on, 'Because if it is to make her feet look like ours, we are quite happy with them as they are, thank you!'

Strange how children find caring so simple, when we as adults somehow seem to make it all so complicated. We need to ask, and continue to ask ourselves, why we expend such effort, go to such lengths, invest such large sums of money and resources, in order to detach some people from the real care and support that freely exists in their own local communities. We do this in favour of a life which can commit children like Lauren to an unnecessary oblivion.

Lauren's mother once commented, 'Prior to integration, I might as well have been pushing an empty wheelchair to the shops.'

It's chilling to think of the restrictions we are placing on the lives of all the other Laurens who even now are kept apart in special schools.

MICHAEL B

Michael came to Overdale School on the day that it first opened. He is an attractive young boy, with an engaging smile. At that time, however, his smile sometimes belied his intention, for he would follow it through by placing his arms around another child, with his face close to theirs as if to kiss them, and would then proceed to bite hard. His behaviour was 'challenging', as they say, and certainly most unpredictable. After two weeks, Michael had made his mark in Overdale School, often quite literally. Staff were already calling for his exclusion. Where they thought he should go was, to me at least, unclear. Had he been a Catholic, he would have been excommunicated; if he had been a wife of Henry VIII, heads would have rolled!

Whilst Michael appeared to be just like any other child (which of course he was), he did in fact have severe learning difficulties and a most aggressive side to him, which bordered upon the pathological. Paediatricians would probably be able to cite some syndrome with a Latin name fifteen syllables long, but among ourselves, Michael was technically referred to as a 'little sod'. His attention span was quite fleeting and just about everything seemed to distract him. He was then just seven years old and, as far as schooling was concerned, he was fast becoming nomadic.

Human services on the whole seem to work as follows. Having determined categories of people and categories of establishments in which to place them, professionals proceed to play a game which I shall call 'pass the pathology'. It is played when a newcomer presents difficulties and does not quite fit in to the routines, upsets the equilibrium of the place and generally causes the service and the professionals some embarrassment or disruption—in short, he does not obviously fit the category allotted to him. The game has simple rules which are easy to learn, and anyone can play it. It is rather like pass the parcel in reverse: one must never hold the package too long, otherwise one will have to unwrap it and look inside. I suppose it is an attractive game, since there are always several winners but only one loser—the loser being the parcel, or the person who is continuously passed round. Of course, this passing on of people is always done on the clear understanding that it is for their own benefit, and when the vast array of assessments, reports and case conferences is concluded, the individual's case is always summarised with a view that his needs should be met *somewhere else*!

When Michael's name was drawn from the hat, we knew that he of all children would really put to the test our philosophy and the feasibility of our pilot study. At the age of seven he was on his third school, and was already in danger of outstaying his welcome at Overdale. I have come across children like Michael many times, and what many of us often fail to appreciate is that, irrespective of any special needs they may

Michael B learning about books with one of his school friends.

have, their behaviour is the normal response that any child would exhibit in the face of experiences such as Michael endured. For all the considerable investment that we put into them, our services sometimes seem to create far more problems than they actually solve. We looked at Michael's statement of special needs again. It was about as illuminating as the proverbial Toc H Lamp.

Section Two (special educational needs):
   Michael has attended a special unit since January 1984 after a period at a Nursery School for children who have severe learning difficulties.
   Michael's progress has been very slow. His strengths appear to be in physical skills and music but his language skills remain limited and have shown relatively little improvement. A major concern is that Michael's awareness is erratic and his level of concentration and recall are low.
   Michael requires an educational environment in which the teaching methods are geared to children who are developmentally young and whose learning difficulties are greater than those of the children in a special unit.

Section Three (provision to meet those needs):
   Michael should follow an individualised learning programme based on a developmental curriculum. He should be taught in a class with a high adult/child ratio.

Section Four (appropriate school or other arrangements):
   Michael should transfer to a school for pupils with severe learning difficulties. Provision will be made at Overdale School.

Section Five (additional non-educational provision):
   Continued speech therapy is required.

So this was Michael's statement of special needs, the piece of paper which was to 'protect' him. It was about as valuable as the one held aloft by Neville Chamberlain in 1938, signed by the Führer. If this was what Michael was being offered, then surely a place in a mainstream school, with full support to meet his needs, would be a vast improvement, despite his anti-social behaviour.

We approached the headteacher of Michael's local main-stream primary school. Even after some discussion, he re-mained anxious about becoming involved. His school was at present undergoing some changes, he explained. For example, the teacher in whose class Michael would be placed was about to be seconded onto a one-year course, and the head did not yet know who would be taking her place. I doubt whether this would have been given as a valid excuse for not accepting any other child into this class, but we did not attempt to argue, as we thought that persuading people to participate in our pilot study against their will would only condemn the child to an unwelcoming atmosphere. On reflection, however, since one of our aims was to change negative attitudes into positive ones, I think perhaps that we should have persisted a little more than we did. Attending one's local school is an import-ant part of being included in one's neighbourhood com-munity. As it was, we followed our agreed procedure and visited the headteacher of the next primary school along. After some preliminary questions, she agreed to discuss the pilot study with her staff and let us know their answer. When it came, this turned out to be in the affirmative, and as I write I am pleased to report that Michael has spent nearly three very happy years there. Discussion is currently taking place to enable him to attend his local secondary school in September.

His primary school has had a remarkable effect upon Mich-ael's behaviour. Almost immediately his frustrated aggression became much less evident and, right from the first day, he has never bitten or even attempted to bite anyone. He joins in all the activities and has made a considerable number of friends. Their behaviour has acted as an excellent yard-stick for his own; being surrounded by so many good examples, all day and every day, has had a very beneficial effect on him. That is not to say, of course, that overnight Michael was converted into a saint, for he certainly was not. Nevertheless, since starting his new school he has neither inflicted injury nor damaged property. Nowadays he has a very pleasant disposition; he shows care for others and of course can also be very cheeky. It is nice to see that at playtimes, when the other children pick sides for a game, he is neither the last nor the first to be chosen. He still has severe learning difficulties and his attention span is still very short, although this too is showing some improvement.

Like all the children in our pilot study, a strong bond has developed between Michael and his classmates. Two years after his placement I visited his class and, without telling them that I was headteacher of Overdale School where Michael had attended previously, I talked to them as a group. Michael himself was not in the room. I asked the children to take a piece of paper and write their own name at the top of it. Then I asked them to imagine that they had been stranded on a desert island and could choose only three others to be with them. I asked them to write down the names of those three others; without discussing their choice and without letting anyone else see. I collected the papers and later was able to map out the sociogramme which appears in Figure 3. Whilst Shelley, Suzanne and Lee stand out as being very popular, Michael's popularity exceeds them all. This is quite remarkable when you consider that he was not in the room that morning and had not been mentioned until then. The same information is portrayed in block graph form in Figure 4 and shows that Michael, even in his absence, polled a total of thirteen popularity votes, six more than Shelley who was next most popular. I encouraged the children to talk about each other in the class, to say what they liked most and what they liked least about each other. After a while, I asked them to tell me about Michael.

'He's got brown hair and brown eyes,' someone started to say.

'No, don't tell me what he looks like, tell me *about* him,' I asked.

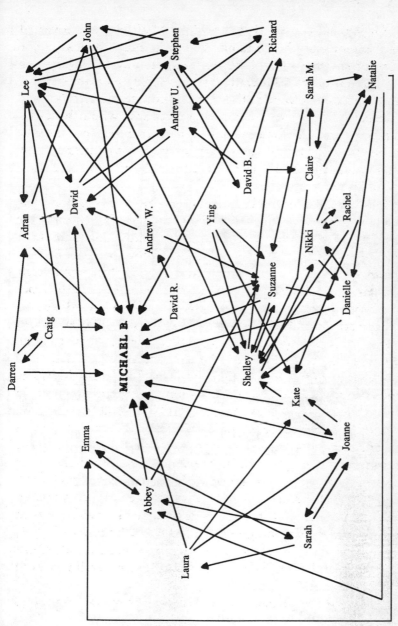

Figure 3. Sociogramme of Michael's class, two years after his placement in a mainstream school.

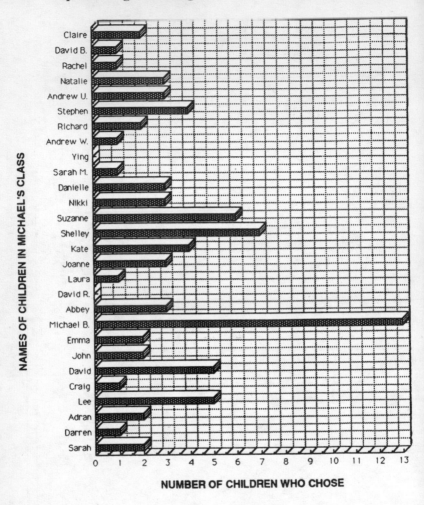

Figure 4. Sociogramme of Michael's class in block graph form.

The next series of statements was made in exactly the following order:

'He's a nice friend to have in the class.'

'He's good to play with.'

'He's funny.'

'He's a good swimmer.'

'He's not all there, a bit backwards.'
'He squeaks his chair a lot.'
'He messes about sometimes.'

This profile more or less matched those that had been given of the others in Michael's class. Interesting, though, that the first four comments were all very complimentary. I am sure that two years earlier, if I had asked the staff at Overdale School to describe Michael, by no stretch of the imagination would they have said that he was a nice friend to have in the class!

I went on to ask the class what they liked most and what they like least about Michael, and recorded the following comments:

LIKED LEAST	LIKED MOST
'He swears (not very often and usually without knowing it')	'He's got a good sense of humour.'
'He taps you sometimes.'	'He's got a nice smile.'
'He goes in people's things without permission.'	'He cheers you up when you're upset and gives you a hug.'
	'He's a good friend.'
	'He likes football.'
	'He's cute.'
	'He's a nice boy.'

It was true to say, therefore, that whilst Michael's severe learning difficulties remained, his anti-social behaviour had greatly improved. There had been no great miracle to bring about this transformation, just the fulfilment of a basic human need—to belong. Michael now not only has friends but is valued and shares a sense of belonging. This was not only essential to his development but easy to provide. If it can be achieved just in the normal course of events by a group of nine-year-olds, it can surely be accomplished by us adults, too.

LIZZIE

When Lizzie's name was chosen at random for our pilot study, it was immediately assumed by some that she would be a non-starter. Their minds were made up even before we had approached the headteacher of her local mainstream school. It was indicative of the attitude that seems to pervade this whole notion of including people who have special needs in the everyday activities and facilities of their local community. Rarely is it due to a deliberate effort specifically to exclude, but more often because those people who 'act on their behalf' compromise for them far too early. The consequences, however, no matter how well-meaning the intentions might be, are always the same: people with special needs end up devalued, discriminated against and segregated.

Lizzie was just two years old in 1988 and she was extremely limited in her movements. She wore a body splint that rather resembled a Roman soldier's breastplate, the purpose of which was to prevent her torso from twisting farther than it already did. Her vision, too, was very poor indeed and she had been given spectacles to wear. In the event, these seemed about as useful to her as a double bed would be to a celibate priest, since she had no blink reflex and did not appear to respond at all to bright light. She did, however, seem to notice the difference in changes from light to dark. Her epilepsy meant that she was prescribed anti-convulsants, which she was given at home each day. She also had an emergency supply of Valium which was to be given rectally should the need arise.

Some people thought that this alone would prevent Lizzie from being offered a place in a mainstream setting, since they felt that nobody would be adequately qualified to cope with this medical responsibility. There was, after all, a fully qualified school nurse appointed to Overdale School for five mornings each week, to deal with conditions like these, so why did she need to be put at risk elsewhere? 'How would ordinary people in a mainstream setting handle this situation?' I was asked, with a self-satisfied, 'get out of that' tone of voice.

Of course, Lizzie would have been very well looked after had there been any such emergencies at Overdale School—well, at least in the mornings. I suppose people must have thought that special needs like hers somehow disappeared in the afternoons and on the way to and from school in the minibus that transported her, and at weekends and during school holidays. The reality was that Lizzie had never actually been in the situation where she needed to be given Valium rectally, so it was not as though we were expecting this to be a daily occurrence. Moreover, administering Valium rectally does not require the services of a top surgeon. Lizzie's mother is totally untrained, but she had been shown how to master this skill in just a few minutes. When you come to think about it, what could be simpler? There is only one small container of Valium and just one place to put it. The target is obvious enough and one does not require the darts prowess of Jockey Wilson to be able to complete the task successfully.

Another worry for some was Lizzie's age. At two she enjoyed full-time education at Overdale School, but no mainstream nursery school was going to give her more than five mornings or five afternoons each week. It is a strange rationale which exists within many Local Authorities, and it goes like this. Children under the age of five years are too young to attend school on a full-time basis. They should be at least three years old before they attend a nursery and even then it should only be on a part-time basis as they will become too fatigued, and in any event they should not be away from their parents for too long. If, however, the same child has severe or even profound learning difficulties, then of course she can attend a school from the age of two or even younger, and on a full-time basis if her parents wish. For some unknown reason, it seems, these children will not tire as easily, nor need to be with their parents so much.

Lizzie's local nursery school did not, as it happened, worry unduly about any of these red herrings. Provided she was going to be supported by a full-time classroom assistant, they could not see why she should not attend their school on a full-time basis and be part of everything they did, even if rectal Valium did need to be administered.

The last time I saw Lizzie in Overdale School, she was positioned on a bean bag, in a circle made up of other children in her class who were just like her. They also were positioned on bean bags surrounding their class teacher who was strumming some chords on her guitar and, with one or two other adults, singing the words to 'The Wheels on the Bus', a song which, if not the actual chart-busting number one of all special schools, surely ranks somewhere amongst the top ten. The adults in the class were singing as enthusiastically as they could; none of the profoundly disabled children were, of course, able to accompany them, so they were singing alone. I never fail to marvel at the way in which people do this in special schools, day after day, week after week, without faltering, regardless of the lack of response they get from the children.

I have to admit that I was more than a little disconcerted when I first visited Lizzie in her new school, only to find her in a circle of children surrounding their teacher, who was strumming the guitar and singing . . . yes, you've guessed it—'The Wheels on the Bus'. There was, nevertheless, a considerable difference. All the other children were singing loudly, and one of them was leaning over to Lizzie and quite spontaneously holding her arms in order to help her perform some actions to the song. The children at this nursery school were so young as to be completely untouched by the adult influence of fear and prejudice. Generally, they were far more concerned about themselves and what they were doing than they were about any of the other children in the class. Lizzie was therefore absorbed into the classroom environment as a completely natural phenomenon, just like any other child, and in that sense was able to experience equal opportunity quite readily, within her classroom community.

While Lizzie attended Overdale School, one of the main aims there was to encourage her to gain head control, as her neck was not strong enough to support her head in a way that would give her a good panoramic view of the world. For some months, with the regular help of a physiotherapist, we had carried out an intensive programme of work with quite poor results. Shortly after her transfer to her local school, we noticed that Lizzie had gained considerable control over her head movements and was actually looking much more mature. This was difficult to understand, after operating such an intensive programme with so little effect, until it was explained that the hustle and bustle of the other children constantly coming and going around her all day had made her twist and turn her head almost continuously to see exactly what was going on. The immobility and quietness of her classmates at Overdale School had not awakened her curiosity and motivation. Since Lizzie has attended this nursery school, some parents have taken an active interest in her needs. Without any encouragement whatsoever, they have formed themselves into a group whose aim it is to accrue enough funding to send her to Budapest in Hungary where, it is hoped, she will be able to benefit from the advice given by people in the Peto Institute.

Some notes taken from the diaries of the specialist teachers and the classroom assistant illustrate typical everyday experiences that confront Lizzie in her local mainstream school.

SPECIALIST TEACHER
May 1988: Katie stroked Lizzie's head, put her head next to Lizzie's saying, 'Shhussh,' when Lizzie was complaining.

June 1988: The children at the nursery school are still crowding round Lizzie. The novelty is definitely not wearing off.

January 1989: Took group for music session, showed them a flute. Children kept putting Lizzie's head straight. Took group in play corner for a musical session with the chime bars. Placed Lizzie on a nearby bean bag, as she

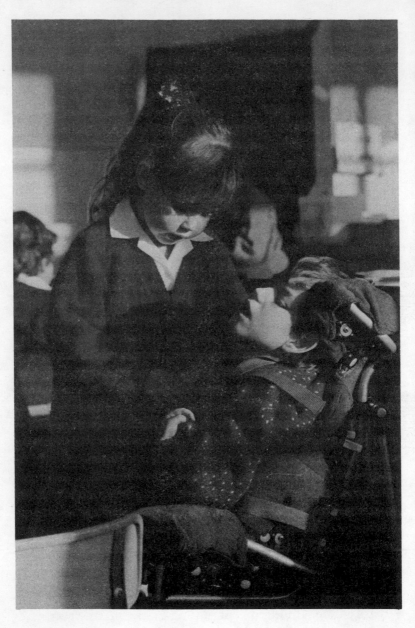

Lizzie with one of her classmates.

seemed too high in her chair. Children automatically played chime bar for Lizzie and tried to put it in her hand. Lizzie laughed in response.

CLASSROOM ASSISTANT
March 1989: The children at the nursery have accepted Lizzie completely from the beginning. Originally there were many questions as to why she could not walk or talk. The children love to be involved in Lizzie's programmes of work, especially the anticipation games, their favourite being the blanket game which ends with all the children, including Lizzie, giggling uncontrollably.

As I write Lizzie is about to leave this nursery school in order to take her place in the local primary school nearby, where she will continue her education alongside the classmates she has come to know over the past two or three years. Her classroom assistant has of course played an absolutely crucial role in fully supporting her special needs in this setting and she will continue to need this degree of support for the foreseeable future, perhaps for the rest of her life. It is exactly this support that will address her special needs in a way that will allow her to be part of the world in which we all live.

PHILLIP

Phillip was seven years old when his name was selected from the 'prize draw', but eight years old by the time he actually started at his local mainstream school.

His statement of special educational needs, received from the Education Authority, read as follows:

Section Two (special educational needs):
   Phillip presents as a pupil with considerable developmental delays.
   He needs:
   1   to develop his expressive language;

2   to recognise a functional core vocabulary of written
     words;
3   to develop and enjoy basic reading skills;
4   to improve his concentration span and eye contact;
5   to develop self-confidence;
6   to improve fine motor skills;
7   opportunities for integration with other pupils.

Section Three (provision to meet these needs):
    Phillip should attend a school for pupils with severe
    learning difficulties and should benefit from:
    1   Specialist tuition in a small group situation.
    2   An individualised, structured educational pro-
         gramme to be devised under the direction of the
         headteacher.

Section Four (appropriate school or other arrangements):
    Phillip should attend Overdale School for pupils with
    severe learning difficulties.

Section Five (additional non-educational provision):
    Phillip's requirements for paramedical services including
    speech therapy and occupational therapy should be
    monitored carefully.

Whilst he had always been regarded as having severe learning
difficulties, academically Phillip was in some ways rather more
able than the others who formed part of our scheme. The infant
school and primary school in the area where he lived were two
separate establishments and were organised quite differently by
the two headteachers who were in charge of them. At the age of
seven or eight, the children who had attended the infant school
were herded across the playground to the junior school
campus. Phillip's birthday placed him on the borderline, so he
attended the infant school for a while, where he gained a great
deal of confidence and a good many friends too.
    The change in his lifestyle was quite staggering. He would

bring friends home to tea after school and in exchange be invited to their homes. Whilst his parents found the opening up of his social life most gratifying, like the other parents who had children participating in our pilot study, for quite a long time, whenever these invitations were received, they seemed to feel the nagging need to telephone the inviter's parents, in order to make absolutely sure that they realised Phillip was handicapped. Invariably the other parents did, and had no misgivings whatsoever about entertaining him. If your child's special needs are always met by services that highlight his differences, I suppose there is little wonder that you become brainwashed into believing that your child needs constant supervision by special people who have a special understanding of all that can go wrong. Phillip's expanded social life therefore took some getting used to, but more by his parents than by him.

Phillip's time at his local infant school proved most beneficial to him and he showed good progress in all areas of his development. When the time came for him to transfer, with the rest of the class to the junior school, like the other supported children on our pilot study he had to ask if he could enter. Attendance at the junior school was of course automatic for all his classmates. During his placement at the infant school Phillip had accomplished all that had been asked of him and more. His speech had improved significantly, he had achieved a good standard in almost every aspect of the school curriculum and he had behaved well. He was also popular with the other children who had all been most supportive. In many ways, it could be argued, he had worked considerably harder than most of his classmates. Nevertheless, Phillip was the only one who had to seek approval for a place that everyone else could take as read. Surely there was more than just a hint of discrimination here, although naturally nobody seemed to recognise it as such.

Before Phillip was able to take his place along with his friends, enquiries were made about him by the head of the junior school to the infant school staff and Hazel, our peripatetic specialist teacher, and myself were asked to give an account of Phillip to the staff of the junior school and to answer questions about him at one of their staff meetings. A further staff meeting was to be held without us and the headteacher of the junior school elected to let us know their decision at a later date. Naturally, Phillip was quite oblivious of all this, but his parents were not and consequently they spent a most anxious time agonising over the outcome. Phillip had done so well, achieved so much; if the answer was going to be 'no', what did he have to do to make it 'yes'?

It was some time before Phillip's parents received a definite answer. They had been given a date by which they would be told, but this had long passed and, despite a number of telephone calls to the school, they were still kept in the dark. The date when all the other children in Phillip's class were to transfer to the junior school was now just a few days away.

The staff at the junior school were faced with what they saw as a dilemma. Their school already had attached to it a unit which specifically housed children who had moderate learning difficulties. There were ten children in this special unit, which was staffed by one teacher and one classroom assistant. For them, the neatest thing to do would be to place Phillip and his support worker in this special unit thus in one fell swoop improving the staffing ratio for all the children there who had special needs. It would answer, too, they said, some of their concerns about the parents who had children in their special unit. These parents had already expressed a wish, some of them quite vehemently, for their children to be included in the main part of the school with support workers.

'What would these parents say if a child whose learning difficulties are not just moderate, but severe, were allowed to be in the main school full-time and with his own personal assistant?' we were asked. 'What's more, if Phillip has severe learning difficulties, then he would be doing well to be taking a place with those who have moderate learning difficulties. Surely it would be too much for him to jump straight into mainstream.'

One way or another, our educational system often seems well geared to presenting children and their families with a whole series of hurdles, over which they must jump before they can be allowed to move to the next stage, which usually turns out to be yet another hurdle. We reminded the junior school staff that Phillip had most successfully spent a long period, full-time, in his mainstream infant school, and that we did not see the point of him going into a special unit to be prepared for integration, when he was already perfectly well integrated. As far as the other parents were concerned, since they were already campaigning to have their children included in the main school, then the pilot study of which Phillip was a part could well provide them with concrete evidence to support their case. We went on to explain that placement in the special unit would defeat the whole object of our pilot study

Phillip with friends in his class.

and would also be to Phillip's detriment. He would simply
revert back into a system which had segregated him in the first
place, highlighted his differences instead of his similarities and
reduced his chances of experiencing an ordinary school life,
and thereby an ordinary childhood.

The junior school agreed, a little reluctantly, to proceed
with Phillip's placement on the basis outlined in our scheme,
and for a time things proceeded quite well. He continued to
show sound educational improvement throughout the curriculum and his social life was as active as ever. Then Phillip's
parents exercised the right that parents have, which was to
change their son's school. He transferred to a Catholic School
where he has remained to this day. Phillip is still thriving and
attaining new goals. He is extremely happy in his new school
where he has many friends and is very much part of all that
goes on. His bubbly personality enables him to make friends
easily and the other children recognise his special needs and are
completely supportive.

Notes in the diary kept by Phillip's classroom assistant
include:

November 1988: In the playground he is always with the
other children, playing in a group and there is mutual
approach to join in the games. At one point, Phillip
picked up some soil, copying the bad example of another
child, but a second child stopped him and cleaned his
hand.

February 1989: I was slightly worried that the other
children would make too much fuss of him, and in fact
they probably did. This was only to be expected and their
curiosity soon wore off. After all, Phillip is a little boy with
quite an engaging personality, and the other children soon
realised that he was not all that different from themselves.
The children in Phillip's class had been primed by their
class teacher. We were not sure if this was a wise move,
because we thought it would draw undue attention to him.

On reflection, though, I personally think it was the best way. There were few questions that showed anything other than natural curiosity. There was no mistrust, fear or ridicule. Phillip has been thoroughly accepted by the other children, who have invited him home for tea, as well as to their birthday parties. He has made some special friends, but he is generally friendly with everyone.

Phillip lives a full life totally involved within his school and local community. Now that he is approaching eleven, we are keeping our fingers crossed that the Education Authority will allow him to continue his secondary education alongside his friends.

MICHAEL M

Michael entered our pilot study at the age of eight. He was and remains a pleasant little boy with a good sense of humour. Despite his difficulty with speech, he socialises well and makes friends easily. Like a number of children who have Down's Syndrome, he has a fairly substantial hearing loss, although recent operations at this time, which placed grommets in his ears and removed his tonsils (not, I hasten to add, at the same time) seemed vastly to improve this problem for him. Whilst he was in attendance at Overdale School Mike received extra weekly tuition from a teacher for hearing impaired children and this continued without any difficulties when he transferred to his local mainstream primary school. Emotionally he is a very stable young person and he seems able to adapt quite readily to new situations and different routines. He already knew and was known by many of the children who attended his local school, as he comes from quite a large family and was used to joining in games played with his brothers' and sisters' friends in the evenings and weekends. In fact, it was these children who could not understand why Mike had to be taken such a long distance away to school, when he could have gone to their school in the first place, which was just a few streets away. Funny, isn't it, how children can sometimes see things much clearer than their older and wiser counterparts?

Since his new school was so close, one of the things that Mike quickly learned was to walk there and back by himself. This meant that he had to develop some road sense and learn how to follow a simple route. While he was at Overdale School, he had been collected by a minibus and driven door to door, the journey taking fifty minutes in the morning and a further fifty minutes in the afternoon, by the time the transport had stopped to pick up all the other children on the way. Now he was able to operate more independently and his confidence grew because of it.

Mike had made a particular friend in his class, who seemed to have some difficulty getting up in the mornings, which meant that he was sometimes late for school. This was not a

good way of winning friends and influencing people as far as the teacher was concerned. To help his friend, Mike decided to make a point of calling for him each morning on the way to school, so that he could act as a reminder to ensure better time-keeping. Punctuality after all, is the politeness of kings. This worked perfectly well for some time and was yet another indication of how the traditional special school system can often deskill children and unwittingly prevent events like this from occurring. I have to confess, however, that there was one occasion when Mike called for his friend and got no reply. So concerned was he that he spent almost an hour hammering on the door and shouting through the letter box, before eventually giving it all up as lost and going on to school without him. Not only did Mike make himself over an hour late, thereby incurring the wrath of his teacher, but he felt really peeved when he discovered that his friend had gone to school by himself and had arrived about an hour earlier.

When he started at his local primary school, Mike was placed in a top infant class of twenty-seven, including nine junior children. He was the oldest in the class. On entering his new classroom, he first of all had to sit on the carpet with the others and answer his name when it was called for registration. This was an immediate culture shock for him; he had never been required to do this in his special school as most of the children in his class had no speech whatsoever. Nevertheless, he looked about him and, with a little prompting, copied the other children and answered his name when called upon to do so. He then prepared himself to face the next obstacle. He did not have to wait long: it was the school assembly, which lasted for twenty minutes and included the whole school. Staff did not remain with children during this period, and his classroom assistant was requested not to stay with Mike unless she felt it absolutely necessary. She therefore stayed close by but out of sight, vigorously chewing at her fingernails and hoping all would be well. The deputy head, who apparently is not given to platitudes, remarked that Mike had been better behaved than the rest of the school.

At this point, I should mentioned that the school is situated in an area renowned for its social difficulties. It was once rumoured that if anyone paid their rent, the police were sent round to find out where they had got the money from! If bullying, ridicule and exploitation was going to take place at all, surely it would be here, in a school like this. But not so. In comparison with Mike's experience in a special school, this was a place rich in social interaction and learning opportunities. He did not need to have individual sessions in gross and fine locomotor skills, for these were happening all around him the whole time. In the playground he soon learned how to run, stop, swerve, twist and turn, and to negotiate a way round other children (particularly those who were much bigger than him). Manipulative skills were practised and reinforced in a classroom where children were constantly using crayons, pencils, paint brushes and a wealth of drawing material. Expressive language was used and needed incessantly where everyone talked at every opportunity—unlike special schools where the silence can be deafening from the children's inability to speak. There was no lack of imaginative play and interaction, with children attempting to model their latest heroes like Superman and ninja turtles. Gangs were formed, friends and enemies, us against them. All the time, preferences were stated and choices applied.

The other children in Mike's class were themselves an added resource. When a new task was introduced, they always wanted to know if Mike would be able to do it too. If he could not, they soon thought of ways in which he could join in, some of them quite ingenious. The one thing Mike disliked most was having to visit his speech therapist from time to time, who was based at Overdale School. Although he chattered constantly to his classroom assistant on the way there in her car, and on the way back, too, he closed like a clam while he was there and said very little at all.

Three years on from the time Mike first went to his local primary school, he is doing all the things that the other children do, sharing in the ups and downs of daily life. He may never become chairman of ICI, Governor of the Bank of England, or even captain of his school's football team, but neither do most people. Still, he will have a full and active life with all the choices, opportunities and status that the rest of us seem able to take for granted.

Mike had spent all his early life in a school for children who have severe learning difficulties, until he began our pilot study. Even so, he had never had, and still has not, a formal written statement of his special educational needs, despite several requests. We organised an annual educational review for him some six months after he had started his placement at the local mainstream primary school. Those present were his mother, the headteacher of the mainstream school, his class teacher, Hazel our peripatetic specialist teacher, Mike's classroom assistant and myself. The summary of Mike's progress read:

> Mike is developing well in all areas of the curriculum. It is generally felt that his placement at his local mainstream primary school has given him opportunity for more social independence. Improvement has especially been noticed in reading, number concepts and pencil skills. Mike has made a lot of friends at his local mainstream school and he is genuinely liked by the children in his class. Improvement has been noted in his auditory skills and his articulation has been clearer since his ear and throat operations earlier this year.
>
> PARENT'S VIEW
> Mike's mother was delighted with her son's placement and progress. She does not want him to return to Overdale School. She stated that she thought that she could now trust him more when he was playing outside.

For Mike, placement within his local school had been as natural as the sun rising in the east. It enabled him to get on with his real life, which we in the past seemed to have interfered with and prevented him from doing by taking him away from his neighbours and his home surroundings. The children in his district already knew him and were supportive. Receiving Mike into their school, where he ought to have been in the first place, seemed to them like a wrong which was at last being put right.

SO FAR SO GOOD

By September 1988 our pilot study had been in operation for five months, which meant that we were approaching its halfway stage. I am pleased to report that all five children from Overdale School remained in full-time attendance at their local mainstream schools. I am equally pleased to be able to say that they all appeared happy and well settled into their new schools and daily routines. At this time we reviewed the project, quite informally, from the points of view of all those who had participated—the children, their parents, their classroom assistants, their teachers and headteachers. These and others were invited to the teachers' centre in order to discuss their feelings and experiences so far.

The Children Themselves

All the children who had in some way been involved, whether they had special needs or not, reaffirmed my own conviction in the principle of inclusive education. More than any other aspect of our pilot study, they showed just how effortlessly integration can work if given the opportunity. Right from the start, interaction between the local mainstream children and those from Overdale School had been perfectly natural and had not needed to be contrived. In all the schools, children openly asked about their new classmate's disabilities and did their best to help them overcome practical difficulties. The mainstream children constantly showed real concern for the children from Overdale and had quickly become a source of solid support which remained firm throughout. Needless to say, we were very pleased to see this happen from the outset of the project but were even more delighted to discover that it did not erode with time. Enthusiasm was not replaced by indifference and caring did not turn into apathy.

After five months of operating this alternative system of special education, I had no doubts whatsoever that all children had benefitted considerably. Those who had severe learning difficulty had gained from having normality brought into their lives, and the children in the receiving mainstream schools had developed a better insight into the needs of those experiencing learning difficulties, who share their world better when they are brought alongside rather than left outside.

The Teachers and Headteachers

We were particularly grateful to all staff in the mainstream schools who had consented to participate in our pilot study. We were only too aware of the difficulties that class teachers have in trying to hear some thirty-six children read individually, whilst simultaneously having to cope with a hundred and one other tasks in their daily routines. We could well understand, therefore, the feeling of panic that must have occurred when they were asked to accept into their classes a child who had severe learning difficulties, especially since most teachers in mainstream schools have little appreciation of exactly what that means or entails. To some, they are the children who make up the remedial groups that some schools have, and it must have been quite a rude awakening when the 'severe' in 'severe learning difficulty' turned out to be appreciably more than chronic dandruff and a problem in understanding the rudiments of square roots. Even the provision of a full-time classroom assistant did not always allay these fears. The teachers' first concern of course, had been that the education of those children already in attendance at the school should not suffer and that the sacred class routine should be disrupted as little as possible.

After five months of operating the pilot study, teachers felt that such fears had largely been vanquished and some understanding had begun to evolve; they now recognised that those who had special needs had the same right as the other children to be in the class. All that we had to ask ourselves was, what would they need to be properly supported and maintained there? Teachers were now saying that they did not feel under any undue pressure from the presence of a disabled child, or even from having his adult support worker based permanently in the classroom. It was satisfying to hear them publicly express the view that the overall benefits for everyone had been very apparent.

There was no denying, of course, that there had been some minor upsets and obstacles to overcome on the way. Every new teaching situation, after all, brings with it some teething problems, but this is indicative of the nature of the field of work in which we are all engaged as educationalists—namely children, of whatever variety. Fortunately, teachers and heads are well experienced in overcoming such difficulties, and positive attitudes will always be a significant factor in the success of a scheme like this one.

The Parents
After five months' full-time operation of our pilot study, none of us had yet discovered any parent of children attending the mainstream receiving schools, who had expressed any severe dissatisfaction with the scheme. On the contrary, many praised their schools for becoming involved, which was most gratifying not only for us, but for the mainstream heads, too. Parents of children in the pilot study were also pleased with the project, and absolutely delighted with the progress their sons and daughters had made since it had begun. Parents know their children much better than anyone else and are the first to recognise any problems, however small they are, so we regarded their continued enthusiasm and active support as a major statement in favour of the scheme, up to this point at least.

I have to say that I sympathised enormously with the parents' somewhat battered feelings. It was they, after all, who had borne the emotional brunt both of this pilot study and of the educational service their children had received before it came into operation. Until this project began their children had to attend a special school some considerable distance away from where they lived. The children, some of them just two years old, had to be up very early each morning (and their parents even earlier) to travel by minibus for over two hours each day, simply to get to school and come home again. Their classmates all had severe learning difficulties, and if they had speech difficulties, as most of them had, they had no chance of hearing normal speech from others around them. Their friends in the special school were certainly unlikely to be in a position to help them in the same way that the children in the mainstream school could.

Whilst this pilot study provided five of our parents with their first real opportunity to have their child attend the local school, it also brought with it some fresh anxieties.

'Will my son be able to cope?'

'Will the other children accept my daughter for who she is, rather than what she is?'

'Will other parents react unfavourably?'

'Shall I suddenly receive a telephone call telling me my child is to be placed back into a special school next week?'

Parents must have been feeling that they were living on a knife edge. The benefits of the project were so obvious to them, the whole situation had been a dream realised. Was it going to prove itself to be just too good to be true? Where was the snag, the fly in the ointment? Would it all soon come crashing down around their ears?

For the first time ever, their children were recognised and greeted by others in the street.

For the first time ever, their children were invited to other children's houses.

For the first time ever, their children wore school uniforms like the other children in their street.

For the first time ever, their children had been treated by others as people in their own right.

For the first time ever . . . the list seemed endless.

The Classroom Assistants

The classroom assistants were and are an essential and integral part of this alternative system of special education. Their ability to deal with the nuts and bolts of our pilot study's infrastructure, on a day-to-day basis, is fundamental in obtaining a desirable outcome. They must be all things to all people and be able to anticipate the problems before they occur. Whilst their job is certainly underpaid, it is by no means undervalued. The task of the support workers is made much easier when they receive the full co-operation of everyone else who is part of the school to which they have been allocated. Cooks, caretakers, cleaners, secretaries, teachers and head-teachers can be helpful or unhelpful, and throughout the five schools included in our pilot study the degree of helpfulness had varied. In certain circumstances, the classroom assistants' role was somewhat isolated, and some of them occasionally felt that they could not identify themselves with either the mainstream school or the special school from which their child had originated. Some, at this stage, also felt that they had a dual allegiance to both their class teacher and to the peripatetic specialist teacher, which must have been quite difficult for them at times. Nevertheless, their contribution formed the backbone of our project.

The Specialist Teacher

Hazel, our specialist teacher, was the scheme's single most valuable asset. At the beginning of her career she had qualified as a teacher in mainstream primary schools and had taught in them for some years. She had also taught more recently within special schools for children who had severe learning difficulties. She was therefore able to relate to the hopes and fears of just about everyone who was involved in the project. She came into our pilot study with an open mind and determined to see that it would have a fair hearing.

Five months on, Hazel was, like myself, totally convinced that inclusive education should be made available for all children who have special needs. For her the most pleasing aspect of the study was the way the children simply got on with each other in a natural, unassuming way. She had discovered, too, that teaching via support workers in this consultancy fashion meant that she had to produce far more individual programmes for each of the children, far more frequently than when she had taught them in a traditional class setting at Overdale. The alternative system of special education allowed classroom assistants to carry out programmes of work with their children at such a rate that Hazel sometimes found it difficult to keep pace with the demand for new material. She told us that her greatest pleasure was to walk into a school and see children who had severe learning difficulties surrounded by the hustle and bustle of everyday classroom activity; on many occasions she had considerable difficulty in picking them out from the rest of the class, particularly when they were wearing school uniforms.

Having reached the halfway point of our pilot study, our specialist teacher, who was the prime co-ordinator, was convinced that the integration she had experienced was not only beneficial to all concerned, but was also entirely compatible with the 1981 Education Act. In 1978, the Warnock Report, when discussing the issue of integration, could foresee the difficulties ahead (after all, nobody said that it would be easy), and they forecast then that 'integration would not be achieved by legislation alone. It must be contrived and patiently nurtured.' This was what was happening and, thanks to all those who were taking part, it was without doubt happening very successfully.

Part Three

EVALUATING THE EXPERIENCE

7   The Findings of the North West Development Team

Whilst Stockport Education Authority had commissioned the Hester Adrian Research Centre at Manchester University to undertake the evaluation of our pilot study, it was the written comments of a review carried out by the North West Development Team that I received first. We had not planned for the pilot study to be examined by anyone other than the Hester Adrian Research Centre, but I was approached quite unexpectedly by Chris Gathercole, who had heard a little of what we were trying to achieve in respect of inclusive education, and he offered to review what we had done and to furnish us with some written observations. Whilst I realised that the Education Authority would not recognise this work as part of their official evaluation, I was pleased to accept Chris's kind offer, as I knew it would be extremely useful to us in seeing whether we had kept as close to our original vision as we had intended. Often, over a period of time, we can make so many tiny compromises that, without realising it, we find that they have crept up on us and accumulated into one big one. Then, if we are not careful, that which we first set out to achieve becomes quite different in the end result. Not only would the North West Development Team review be a good gauge for us, it would also be a trifle more independent than the official evaluation, since the team members were not being paid by the Education Authority for their efforts.

At the time there was some concern from education officers at my agreement to this review. There was a feeling that it might contaminate the official evaluation which was to be carried out by the Hester Adrian Research Centre if the latter were to read it before writing their own document. I contacted Manchester University and was reassured by them that a second written observation would not affect their own findings in any way; in the event, they would not be reading it before completing their own document. I have therefore, with their permission, included in this publication a copy of the North West Development Team's findings, interjected with my own comments.

Some Quotations About the Pilot Study

'He's a privilege to know . . . The whole school has benefited by having him—the other children and teachers . . . I'm glad he's staying with us. *Headteacher*

'It's fantastic the way he's coming on.' *Mother*

'Stockport is committed to educating as many children with special needs as possible in ordinary schools.' *Stockport Metropolitan Borough Education Division. Information For Parents—1989/90*

'Selling integration is hard work.' *Peripatetic Specialist Teacher*

'I had some doubts at first, but now I'm convinced it's right.' *Teacher*

'It's all to do with the attitudes of all concerned.' *Headteacher*

'Academically he's not that great, but his social behaviour is a treat.' *Classroom Assistant*

'Her presence has had no detrimental effects on the learning processes of the other children; on the contrary, it was felt to be most beneficial and advantageous.' *Minutes of school staff meeting*

'I think it's been a very successful experiment. I'm delighted with it.' *Headteacher*

INTRODUCTION

This review of the Overdale integration project was arranged in order to learn from the experience of one of the most significant examples in Britain of a systematic approach to transferring children from segregated school to mainstream school. Despite increasing interest in the 1970s and 1980s in integration in education for children with special needs, there has been little effort on behalf of children with severe learning difficulties. There are some examples, often where parents have fought the educational establishment against great odds. It seems that there is a widespread view that integration is to be taken seriously for children with other special educational needs, but not for children with severe learning difficulties.

There have been major changes in Health and Social Services in Greater Manchester and Lancashire, towards enabling people with learning difficulties to take their place in the life of the community. Children are no longer admitted to long stay hospitals. The long stay hospitals are scheduled for closure and a major resettlement programme is currently in progress. Adult Training Centres are changing their ways of functioning, so that opportunities for supported employment in real work are now growing. There has been substantial growth in opportunities in Further and Adult Education. At the pre-school stage, too, many children are integrated in nurseries and playgroups.

The last major frontier for integration, then, is mainstream schooling for 5–16-year-olds. A special school which takes the initiative in aiming to end its role as a special school is rare in Britain, although elsewhere (Ontario, Canada, for example) whole districts have already shut all special schools for children with learning difficulties, by placing them in ordinary classes in mainstream schools.

The visiting team of four people consisted of Chris Gathercole, Development Team member and clinical psychologist; Brian Eckersley, whose foster daughter has severe learning difficulties and attends a special school in Tameside near

Manchester, where he is a school governor; Jenny Taylor, who teaches in a school for children who have severe learning difficulties; and Joe Whittacker, who is responsible for training teachers in further education, concerned with students who have special needs, including those with severe learning difficulties.

The visit involved a half-day briefing by Kenn Jupp, Overdale's headteacher, and Hazel Quinn, the peripatetic teacher who supports the five children placed in mainstream schools. The team spent an afternoon with parents of three of the children in the project. Each of the five schools was visited by a team member who met the heads, class teachers, classroom assistants, and all the children except one who was in hospital at the time. We looked at the files kept on each child by the classroom assistants, recording progress on the teaching programmes. We also looked at the diaries kept by classroom assistants and the peripatetic teacher.

This review took place in March 1989, at the end of the first twelve months of the project, which began in April 1988.

DEGREES OF INTEGRATION

The term 'integration' has been applied loosely to a variety of arrangements. Functional integration refers to the fullest degree of contact with non-handicapped children in ordinary schools. This may involve the provision of support within the classroom from an extra classroom helper. The aim is to include the handicapped child in as many of the regular activities of the curriculum as possible.

Locational integration refers to arrangements in which a handicapped child is taught on the campus of a mainstream school, but in a separate class or unit. The class or unit may be physically within the main building, or separate.

Social integration refers to contact of handicapped and non-handicapped children outside lessons, at meals and playtimes, for example.

The Overdale project aimed at the fullest degree of functional integration possible, without exclusion on the basis of disability or behaviour difficulty.

OUTCOMES

At the time of the visit, all of the children were better known in their own communities and neighbourhoods than at the start of the project, not only by local children, but by adults as well. They were greeted in the street more and invited into other children's homes more.

> 'She was shipped off to another district every day and brought back, so nobody saw her or knew who she was. But now, everybody knows who she is and they all say hello to her . . .'
>
> *Classroom Assistant*

Three of the children were learning some of the social rules which assist social acceptance: following instructions, being quiet at appropriate times, standing still when the whistle is blown, lining up. One child was quite disruptive in school assembly at the start: shouting, waving his hands, shuffling about, but is much better now. One boy had learned to make other children laugh by silly clowning; this is much improved so that he is acting more sensibly now. One had temper tantrums at the start, but these are rare now.

One was concentrating attention on a single task and sitting for up to three-quarters of an hour, whereas at the start his limit was said to be five seconds.

Eye contact with one child has improved. She is acting more alertly to situations and giving signs of greater understanding.

One profoundly handicapped child was showing active interest in what was going on around her, whereas at the start she was described as bland and passive. Another child, also profoundly disabled, developed head control within weeks of starting at the mainstream school.

One child had a reputation for biting other children at Overdale, mainly smaller and more vulnerable ones. After the first week at his new school, there have been no reports of biting at all.

Three children are making progress in academic work: number, reading and writing. One has much improved verbal communication.

Each of the children has made significant progress which probably would not have happened if they had not been taking part in the project. Most of the improvements cannot be firmly attributed to the change of school. We do not know whether similar improvements might have been made if the children had stayed at Overdale. This seems most unlikely, however, as they are being challenged far more in their present schools, with far more personal tuition and models of non-handicapped children to imitate.

Despite the progress, each child continues to have severe learning difficulties. It should not be inferred that because of some striking improvements, the children have miraculously put aside their disabilities.

The degree of functional integration within the classes of the schools varies, depending on the level of functioning of the children and the interest of the class teachers. All of them are socially integrated at dinner times, play times and school assemblies.

There have been benefits to other children in the schools. Genuine reciprocal friendships have developed. An acceptance of children who are different in some way has been taken in their stride. Of course, this should not surprise us. It is often observed, especially with primary school children, that they do not have the prejudices which beset adults. As one class teacher said,

'My generation have got more hang-ups than these children will ever have.'

As far as we could tell, there has been no bullying. Indeed, we learned of several examples of children demonstrating a sense of responsibility and caring, not in a sentimental or pitying way, but with a sense of proper concern for their fellow human beings. One boy with a reputation for being tough and rowdy, has made it his business, without being asked, to go through class work with a child with learning difficulty.

A worry expressed by parents before the project started was whether the children would be mocked and derided, but no incidences of this have been observed so far. In one school, a boy gets picked in games to be in a team, even though the children know their side is likely to lose when he plays for them.

On the down side, one or two children have taken advantage of children easily led astray. Two girls, for example, persuaded a child with learning difficulty to roll in the mud for a joke. Another child was persuaded to dance in the school assembly, when he was supposed to be sitting still.

Parents of the project children are all delighted with how things have turned out. They may have been a little uncertain at the start, but now would resist fiercely any attempt to go back to segregated provision. Mums have got to know their local Mums through their children, for example, by chatting at the school gate.

Parents of classmates in the mainstream school also seem to be positive about their children being in a class with a child having severe learning difficulty. We heard of no objections whatsoever from such parents. Parents of project children were initially worried that parents of other children in mainstream schools might object to having a handicapped child being taught with their non-handicapped children. This has not happened, indeed, some parents have expressed delight with the opportunity their child has had of meeting a handicapped child.

All the teachers of the mainstream classes which took a child seem to have surprised themselves at how positive they have become about it. One or two were apprehensive at the start, but all now feel it has been a worthwhile experience for themselves, as well as for the children. One reported that she had been led to rethink some of her teaching methods through contact with the child with learning difficulty in her class.

Several were surprised with the level of abilities of the children they received. Initially they had very low expectations. Most of the class teachers were not sure how to treat the project children. How much allowance should be made for them? It did not take long before they were treating them like the others in the class.

Having another adult in the class was difficult at first for one or two teachers, but this was something they had become used to over the year. Indeed, several had found the extra person in the classroom particularly helpful for work with other children.

All the classroom assistants felt the project had been worthwhile and they enjoyed their work, although they have had some difficulties. The low salaries and poor conditions of service were problems for most.

The headteachers, and most other class teachers not directly involved, were positive about the project. The heads unanimously stated that it could not have been done without the classroom assistants. All insisted that if the project were to remain viable, they needed reassurance that the classroom assistants would stay and would not be financed from their existing school resources.

We did hear of one class teacher who refused to consider accepting a project child when the time came for going up into the next class.

Comment

This particular class teacher expressly refused to teach a child who had severe learning difficulties. If she had wanted to teach such children, she pointed out, then she would have trained to teach within the field of special education in the first place. This same teacher confided that, on a personal basis, she found such children rather repulsive and because of this, did not feel that she would be able to get close enough to them to teach them properly. This teacher had such strong feelings that she threatened to hand in her notice if the supported child was given a place in her class. Whilst we felt this behaviour constituted a flagrant example of discrimination, the education officer ruled that in situations like this teachers should be allowed to have the right of refusal. If these guidelines are to be widely implemented, I wonder what will happen when teachers start to declare an aversion to children with red hair, or those who wear glasses. I pondered, too, on what would happen if the pretty little girl who sat at the front of this particular teacher's class should burn herself badly one day; would the teacher refuse to take her back into the class, and would the education officer still support this action?

I am pleased to be able to write that, shortly after our child started there, this same teacher began to recognise the similarities that this supported child had with all the other children in the school. As time went on, this teacher found that she had no objection at all, and a year later, she was quite happy to have our supported child in her class. A year after that, however, when it was time for the child to move on yet again, the class teacher had become quite possessive and showed great reluctance in letting the child go. Ironically, this teacher's attitude had swung from one extreme to another, neither of which was particularly beneficial.

These findings have to be qualified by the limitation of our visits. The Hester Adrian Research Centre will no doubt have more detailed information on which to base conclusions. Nevertheless, we can conclude that the goals of the project have been met. Five children with a range of learning, physical and social difficulties have been successfully integrated into mainstream schools, to the satisfaction of all directly involved. The common fears expressed by parents, teachers and others, when integration is proposed, have not proved justified. What difficulties there have been have largely concerned the attitudes of the adults. Few have been to do with the children themselves.

INGREDIENTS FOR SUCCESS

The project was well planned and well organised from the start. Careful preparation and groundwork was done. All the people involved have been very capable and are to be commended: Kenn Jupp in seeing the opportunity, taking the initiative and guiding it through every stage with care; Hazel Quinn, who had experience of primary school teaching and understands both primary and special schools, in getting the support of heads and teachers as well as supervising the classroom assistants; the classroom assistants themselves; and the parents for their support. All contributed to ensuring the project worked for the children concerned.

The more an individual-centred approach is adopted in the mainstream class, the more effectively and easily is a child with special needs incorporated.

All along, Kenn Jupp and Hazel Quinn have been sensitive to the concerns raised by anyone involved.

'The whole thing was like walking on eggshells with everybody. We knew people would feel threatened, so it forced it into our heads that we were guests in the schools. As time has gone on, as relationships have built up, that's been less of a problem.'

CHALLENGES FOR THE FUTURE

The main challenge for the future is how to safeguard the fragile but highly significant progress made so far, and how to extend the project so that every child with severe learning difficulty in Stockport can have the same opportunities as non-disabled children.

One way forward would be to form a group including parents, teachers and anyone else interested in developing integration in education. We learned that all the participants in the project felt somewhat isolated. Support was available individually, but what is needed is for people to have the opportunity to come together more, so as to feel part of a wider movement. A group such as this would provide an open forum for discussion of integration issues and could contribute to raising awareness of the benefits of integration and dissemination of the lessons learned from the past year. The central task of such a group would be to change the climate of opinion. At present the climate is mainly not supportive of integration for children with severe learning difficulties. Those with direct personal experience of its benefits, including parents, teachers and heads, have a major part to play in changing the climate to be more receptive. They can challenge the usual assumptions and low expectations in meetings and personal contacts. They can question the status quo whenever the opportunity arises. If those most closely concerned won't speak up on behalf of our most needful children, who will? For example, it is not widely appreciated that, at primary school level, there would average one or fewer children with severe learning difficulties per school, if all were dispersed into their local neighbourhood schools. On average, there is one such child in about 250 children.

Comment

This is certainly true. Any small project which takes a leap in the dark, like this one, no matter how successful it may be, still needs a strong structure of like-minded people around it, who celebrate the achievements and encourage others to join its network of support. Alternative systems like this cannot be built around just one or two people, they must develop in such a way that the system can stand by itself. This means that people from all walks of life need to be made aware of the underlying philosophy in recognising that everyone belongs.

Everyone, therefore, has a role to play. It is like adding cement to the bricks when parents share their experiences with other parents and support each other in their quest to obtain what they want for their children. It is also essential for them to make their feelings known to the Education Authority through its headteachers, education officers, members of the Education Committee and Members of Parliament. The Passport Group which emerged from Overdale School has done this particularly well, but they should be joined by staff from both mainstream and special schools. People must stand up and be counted. Between them they can begin to explain to others around them the rationale by which they are trying to operate. Things like financial donations and gifts of equipment should only be accepted if they do not compromise the dignity of the people for whom they are intended. Second-hand, broken toys given to special schools at Christmas time, or the offer of a 'party for the handicapped children' from the local women's group, with the best will in the world actually tell the onlooker that these poor children are needy and that these wonderful, benevolent people are being kind. Whilst the act itself is of course well-intended, the givers obtain a platform for themselves with a spotlight to give maximum illumination to their 'creditable' action, at the direct expense of the receiver who is similarly highlighted as the object of charity.

An early task for the group might be to arrange an event in, say, September 1989, to hear from the five people from the North West due to attend the Summer Institute on Integration in Education at McGill University, Montreal, in July 1989.

Comment
This we did and found it extremely useful. These summer schools, I understand, are run each year for two weeks and are highly regarded by all those who have participated. Anyone requiring further information should contact Joe Whittacker at the Bolton Institute of Further Education, or John Hall at Dyfatty School, Swansea.

The implications of the project for all children with severe learning difficulty in Stockport, including those in other special schools, as well as children placed outside the Borough, need to be considered. If every child is to have the same opportunities, at some point a working group within the Authority will be needed. One early priority for such a group would be to facilitate the entry of new starters into ordinary nursery schools and reception classes in mainstream schools. This would require detailed discussion with the Child Development Unit so that parents are orientated towards the idea of ordinary schooling from the start. A major reason for giving new starters priority is that there is considerable pressure to fill the places vacated by the five project children from Overdale. Unless a policy is developed, it is likely that those places will be filled by children who otherwise would not have been considered for special school, thus extending segregation, rather than curtailing it.

Comment
This was a useful point made by the North West Development Team and is discussed in Chapter 11.

Opportunities for training in the ideas underpinning integration should be available to all concerned. It is important that staff, parents and governors understand the damage which segregation does and the benefits sought from moving to integrated provision. This will help the planning and design of the practical arrangements, so that changes are made in the most effective ways possible. If those most closely involved are not persuaded of the value of integration and are not familiar with the principles, there is a possibility of changes being made in a half-hearted way. So far, the commitment of all concerned has carried the project through successfully, but if it is to be extended, safeguards for quality will be needed as more people are involved and as the novelty wears off. The transition from small-scale demonstration project to large-scale change requires special attention. It is not just a question of doing more of the same. The need to maintain the standards set by the original project should be a central aim. Orientation to the values which support integration is best done through training, which includes a mix of people from different backgrounds and agencies. Already there is a tradition of Health, Social Services and voluntary bodies co-operating in this way, but unfortunately, nationally, as well as locally, education has consistently not been a part of that tradition.

Comment
This too is discussed in Chapter 11.

One detail of the project process concerned us. A major aspect of integration in education is to assist children's integration in their neighbourhood, outside school hours. One child was not able to go to the first choice local primary school but was transferred to the second choice school which was a little farther away and required a bus journey (public transport) to get there. This meant that he did not get to know children in the immediate neighbourhood of his home and, consequently, did not get invited to play or to birthday parties.

If the scheme is extended and the random selection procedure continued, we recommend that only the local school be approached for each name taken from the hat. If that does not work out, then another name should be selected. This means that if there are any children unable to go to their neighbourhood schools, they will have to wait until last. Depending on how long the whole process takes, there will be time for the preferred schools to adjust to the idea.

It might be argued that schools have no right to reject children; however, it is obviously much better if they take children willingly and it has to be recognised that some will take longer than others to come round to positive acceptance. The examples of success from the project so far should help to reassure any doubters.

Comment
This part of the report worried us. It is of course true that taking a second choice school meant that this child did not develop a network of friends outside school like the others on our pilot study. It is also true to say that attending one's local school is vital to the process of inclusion. By building a second chance into the project we thought we were safeguarding the children's interests. In reality, this part of the report made us aware that we had compromised. Compromising is always dangerous and, if done at all, should only be a last resort. We had made the assumption that this child would have better life opportunities by being integrated into a mainstream school, albeit one outside his immediate locality, rather than remaining in a segregated special school like Overdale. The child concerned has undoubtedly benefited considerably from his three years in a mainstream school, far more than he ever would if he had remained in Overdale. Neverthe-

less, this has meant that another child, who perhaps would have experienced even greater and longer-lasting benefits by being placed in a school within his own home environment, has been denied the opportunity. On reflection, we should, I think, have pressed harder for the first choice school to agree to participate, even though they might initially have shown extreme reluctance. Our experience, in the light of our pilot study, tells us that these poor attitudes would probably have changed quite dramatically in a fairly short time.

A similar change faces the project when children are scheduled to move up a class or change from infants to juniors or primary to secondary. It is important for a child to move up through school with his age peer group. What happens if a teacher refuses to accept him? Again, one can ask if they have the right to discriminate in this way. One of the reasons why people are rejected is that they are seen as different in some way. If services add to the difference by the way they are delivered, they are contributing further to the likelihood of rejection. It is essential, therefore, that any practice which contributes to a child being seen as different should be reviewed.

—Can a child fit into the school curriculum that the other children are pursuing? Some of the time, project children joined in what the rest of the class were doing, such as PE and music. Mostly, however, they were seen as needing special separate work and teaching. We concluded that sometimes a child could be doing the same kind of work as the other children but was unnecessarily being kept separate.

Comment
A very fair point. The problem with working in the field of special education for so long, and in such a segregated way, is that we reach a stage where we become conditioned into believing our own propaganda, like the need to adopt 'special' activities for 'special' children.

What is really needed is support to enable these children to carry out ordinary activities in ordinary situations. The mysticism created by some specialist teachers leads staff in mainstream schools to believe that teachers in special schools are either an elite band who have acquired fundamental teaching abilities far beyond the norm, or that they are people who have failed to make the grade in mainstream schools and are therefore only capable of teaching less able children.

—Some children had been put into classes with younger children, partly so that they would be more likely to join in. This will increase the ever-present risk, for people with learning difficulties, of being seen and treated as younger than they really are. It could also mean that they are marked out in the process. One boy, for example, was physically bigger than most of his classmates because he was older.

Comment
This also is a very valid point. Whilst we were fully aware of the ideals surrounding the notion of age-appropriateness, we again, I suppose, allowed ourselves to compromise too early. In our defence, however, I would point out that even now the climate in schools generally, for integrating children who have special needs, is somewhat lukewarm; three years ago, when we began to suggest total inclusion, it was positively polar cap temperatures. The whole idea was so threatening to some schools that we had tremendous difficulty in getting past their front door. In consequence, we were treading so carefully at that time that we acceded to their wish for some children to be placed in classes slightly below their chronological age. I am pleased to report that these children are now all attending classes composed of children of their own age, whatever their degree of disability. At the time, however, we felt that the mainstream school itself needed to go through this learning process, with a little help from us, of course.

I would add that it is sometimes hard for a school to take on a child who has severe learning difficulties, when its own previous experi-

ence has been to accept statemented children, only to find what little support it had been given withdrawn by the Authority shortly afterwards. We did not think, therefore, that it would be reasonable to ask a school to participate in our pilot study and expect to dictate the precise terms on which it should operate. The local school, as the child's most immediate local community, should surely be allowed to manage its own affairs and to develop its own system of support, without fear of outside influences either from ourselves or from the Education Authority. Our main task was to ensure that the main-stream school understood the ideas behind Normalisation, so that it could tackle the child's needs in its own individual but informed way.

—Some self-help skills, such as doing up coat buttons, could be more appropriately learned at home.

—Some activities might be disguised as part of the daily routine. For example, one child used a standing frame at times during the day. Would it be possible for her to be held upright while a group of children were listening to a story?

—One child was taken out of class and school to attend riding and swimming lessons, but no other children in the class or school had this opportunity. Could these activities be arranged after school or at weekends so as not to mark the child out as different?

—Some children were taken out of class and returned to Overdale School for speech therapy. How could this activity be arranged so as not to draw such attention?

Comment

Occupational therapists, physiotherapists and teachers of children with hearing impairments are largely peripatetic, and so we had no difficulty in arranging visits to children within their mainstream school on a regular basis. The District Speech Therapist, however, took the view that her service did not have enough resources for her to allow individual speech therapists to visit children in schools other than special schools. We did ask that the children in our pilot study be given the same opportunity as the other children in the mainstream schools who were served from the local clinics, but this was denied us. We had no option, therefore, but to take the children to visit the speech therapist in Overdale School from time to time, in order to get advice.

—The presence of a classroom assistant could be a barrier to incorporating a child into the class; it could also facilitate the process of integration if she was seen as a resource valuable to the whole group and was recognised as a staff member of the primary school.

Comment
This is another very valid point. We did in fact encourage all schools to operate in this way, but at the end of the day, the decision regarding deployment of staff and resources had to be theirs.

—Any special school practices should be rethought in terms of the culture of the ordinary primary school, before transplanting them. Structured teaching, for example, using behavioural methods and arbitrary reinforcement, might be used in conjunction with experiential 'learning by doing' approaches. This requires good judgment on when to use which approach if they are to blend effectively.

Comment
This is so true. I can recall one child who, while he was at Overdale School, had a programme designed for him to learn how to wash and dry his hands after going to the toilet. As with all good special school programmes, the task had been broken into very easy steps (in this case no less than 27), so that the child could not fail as he passed from one stage to the next to achieve the stated goal. He learned the skill, of

course, but the whole painstaking process took him a good many minutes each time he went to the lavatory, and no doubt at Overdale School a member of staff stood there policing him whilst this ritual was carried out. I was more than a little amused, therefore, to see children in the mainstream school, at the end of their lesson time, being told by their teacher to visit the toilet en masse and, under her gaze, taking no more than just a few seconds to run their hands under the tap, mostly being shoved on by the child behind them, and, after the briefest attempt to dry them on paper towelling, rushing off into the playground for their break time. The boy from Overdale was quite bemused at first, but it did not take him long to fall into the ways of the new regime, which must have left him wondering what all the fuss had been about before. Programmes are a buzz word in special schools, but in my view are better applied to computers than they are to children.

—Because a decision has not yet been made about the future of the project, the five children are on Overdale's roll. Their statements are said still to indicate that Overdale is considered the most appropriate provision for their education, even though all concerned are convinced that their present integrated provision is far more appropriate.

Comment
Incredible as it might seem, after several attempts over the past three years to change the statements to indicate that these children are in fact attending their local mainstream school and should therefore be on the roll of that school, the situation remains unchanged, despite a verbal recommendation from a member of Her Majesty's Inspectorate.

Much of the success of the project has been due to the work of the classroom assistants and the way they have fitted in with their class teachers. This success in turn emerges from the way they were selected and their supervision by Hazel Quinn.

However, there are unresolved problems concerning salary and conditions of service. Their title of 'classroom assistant' belies their work, which certainly includes teaching. This contradiction is a puzzle. Their role as teachers, albeit supervised, is essential. Class teachers would not be able to give the individual attention needed by the children. If the classroom assistants were restricted to providing physical care, the project would not work. Their job title permits them to be employed on very low salaries, and indeed three have already left because of this. Such exploitation is unacceptable. It would be desirable for their contracts to be made permanent.

The classroom assistants have had to rely on good will from the other primary staff to obtain coffee and lunch breaks. They remain 'on call' throughout the day.

Comment

The report was quite right to include this observation. After all, it is nonsense for us to be attempting to liberate one devalued group by creating yet another. Classroom assistants are usually underpaid by most, if not all Education Authorities. One reason is that they are easily come by. It is an attractive proposition for many people who have young children, to be able to have a job which only requires attendance during school hours and term time. Education Authorities therefore have very little difficulty in finding personnel to work for this low rate of pay. As far as their title is concerned, at the start of our pilot study we did ask the Authority to refer to them as 'tutorial companions', but this was not taken up, on the grounds that the term 'tutorial' might, and I emphasise might, be objected to by the teaching unions. Classroom assistants undoubtedly do carry out a good deal of teaching and their day-to-day judgements make their presence vital to the success of inclusive education. Perhaps now, with the emergence of 'licensed teachers', and with schools becoming responsible for the management of their own budgets, heads will both see the need and be in a position to implement the upgrading of classroom assistants to licensed teacher status. As far as breaks are concerned, all classroom assistants in special schools normally take their coffee breaks (such as they are) in the classroom and are given

*between half-and-hour and three-quarters of an hour for lunch. Our
pilot study staff operated under these same conditions initially, but we
pointed out to headteachers of the mainstream schools that they would
operate under their own schools' daily routines as determined by them,
not under Overdale's.*

This document of observations made by the North West
Development Team was extremely useful to us. It was written
by people who shared our vision and were not afraid to let us
know where they thought we had fallen down in achieving
our aims. We were greatly encouraged by the overall reassurance it gave us, that we were embarking on our journey in
the right direction, and it was critical enough for us not to
become too complacent about everything we had been doing
so far. It became the central document around which we had
many conversations, both with members of the team and
within our own project personnel. We are fortunate to have
such a group within our part of the country and I thank them
for their valuable contribution to our efforts.

8   The Findings of the Hester Adrian Research Centre

The work for the Hester Adrian Research Centre was carried out by Tricia Sloper and Colin Elliot to whom I should like to take this opportunity to express my thanks, firstly, for taking on the project at all, and secondly, for the professional way in which the whole commission was conducted. I should also like to offer my appreciation to Cliff Cunningham who was a prime facilitator in getting the Hester Adrian Research Centre to take on this evaluation.

From the outset, their report emphasises, 'It must be noted that it is not possible to prove the success or failure of the project within such an evaluation.'

Comment
Whilst this may be the case academically, on a more practical basis, the very fact that the original five children remained full-time in their local mainstream schools throughout and beyond the pilot study was success in itself for those who were directly participating.

The report also underlines the fact that 'The results of a study of this size cannot be generalised to other children or situations. Thus, the study cannot prove or disprove the case for the general integration of children with severe learning difficulties into mainstream schools.'

Comment

Nobody could justifiably argue with this. A sample of just five children is far too small to generalise to others. Nevertheless, the fact remains that five children chosen at random, all with a range of severe learning difficulties, took up their place in their local schools and are still there to this day.

ATTITUDES OF STAFF

The Personal Questionnaire Rapid Scaling Technique (PQRST (Mulhall, 1978)) was used to assess attitudes of heads and class teachers in mainstream schools before the project commenced and again one year later. Thus changes in attitude could be monitored. The administration of this measure was undertaken by MSc students who were completely independent of the pilot study. In addition to this, a questionnaire was devised to investigate attitudes of all staff in the mainstream schools, which was carried out a year after the project commenced.

It was noted from this questionnaire that 43 per cent of the staff's original concerns were entirely dispelled by the end of the pilot study and overall scores on concerns had decreased. This would suggest a diminishing in anxieties and the development of more positive attitudes towards integration as a result of the project. One of the most common worries people had prior to the pilot study's commencement was concern about the acceptance of those children who had special needs by the children already based in the mainstream schools. This was no longer registered as a worry at the later assessment and illustrates how the practical experience of inclusive education had allowed heads and class teachers to reassess their thoughts, culminating in a more positive attitude.

Further questionnaires were given to other staff of mainstream schools involved with the pilot study, including staff such as caretakers and kitchen assistants, and again these

demonstrated mainly positive attitudes. A 67 per cent response rate was obtained and, of these, 72 per cent felt that the
project had been a success and that they personally had gained
from it. Only 6 per cent did not feel that the results had
justified the costs; 62 per cent thought they had and 32 per cent
were undecided, as they were not sufficiently aware of what
costs were involved. The rather low response rate (67 per cent)
does raise the question of whether those who failed to respond
had more negative attitudes. Evidence from the records of
classroom assistants and the specialist teacher, however, suggests that this may not be the case. Negative attitudes in
certain schools were identified as a problem in the early stages
of the pilot study, but it was noted that this problem decreased
over time and attitudes became more positive.

Comment
*I am surprised that the evaluators consider a 67 per cent response rate
to be low.*

ATTITUDES AND BEHAVIOUR OF THE
MAINSTREAM CHILDREN

This appears to be one of the most positive aspects of the pilot
study. Early in the project, the specialist support teacher noted
that, for children in the 'host' schools, 'acceptance was immediate without any intervention from adults', and that 'adults
are the problem, not children'. At the end of the pilot study,
the specialist teacher again notes that the most rewarding
aspect was the other children's attitudes. Many examples are
noted in the dairies that were kept and the reports made
throughout the pilot study, of the help, friendship and acceptance offered towards the children who have severe learning
difficulties. Some of these examples are recorded as follows:

GENERAL OBSERVATIONS FROM THE SPECIALIST TEACHER
September 1988: Right from the start, interaction between

the local mainstream school children and those from Overdale has been quite natural and unforced. In all the schools, children asked direct questions about their new classmates' disablements and, in all schools, direct answers were given, which proved to be the most satisfactory arrangement for all concerned. The children in the mainstream schools have offered genuine help, friendship and encouragement to those from Overdale. At first, I rather expected the novelty of the new situation to wear off and that their initial enthusiasm would be replaced by indifference. This has not happened to date.

April 1989: On the subject of other children, this has been the most rewarding aspect of the whole scheme. The Overdale children have made friends and been genuinely liked by the other children in the classes. The situation has provided endless opportunities for discussion and learning and I have been bowled over by the sensible concern and commonsense questions and ideas that have come from children. Integration, on the children's level, just takes place without any interference from us! I would love my own children to have such a rich experience in their own primary school.

Class teachers and headteachers also commented on the benefits of the pilot study to the mainstream school children, in increasing their awareness and positive attitudes towards disability and their sense of caring. No staff felt that there had been any detriment to mainstream pupils.

Effects on the Social Contacts of the Integrated Children

No social isolation in school was reported in any of the interviews. Most parents stated that social relationships with mainstream pupils went beyond school: children were invited to parties, were greeted at the shops and in the street, where previously they had been ignored, and they played out with friends. However, for the one child who was not attending his local school, no such social carry-over from school to home was reported. The data from the social contacts questionnaires confirm these reports. Three of the four children attending their local schools had increased their amount of contact with neighbourhood children during the project. All four sets of parents were dissatisfied with this aspect of the children's lives before the pilot study, but were somewhat or very satisfied after the pilot study. The exception to this was the child who did not attend his local school. He had fewer contacts with school friends outside school and his parents were dissatisfied. This underlines the importance of consideration being given to the possible effects of out of area school placement.

Comment
This point is also made in the report from the North West Development Team. We certainly should have persisted with this child's placement into his local school.

PROGRESS AND BEHAVIOUR
The progress of individual children participating in the pilot study was examined by consulting review reports, using behaviour problems questionnaires and assessment data. The findings may be summarised as follows:

The three ambulent children, who have severe learning difficulties but who are not profoundly disabled, appear to have shown particular improvement in independence and self-help. It is notable that the mainstream school routine allowed and encouraged considerably more independence than the special school routine, in such matters as dining, toileting and playtime. Concentration, cognitive development and language have also improved for these children, although the decreased use of Makaton may be a disadvantage for one child. The increase in the number of work programmes completed by the children is noted by the specialist support teacher. This may be attributable for the increased one-to-one attention afforded by the provision of a full-time classroom assistant for each child.

The two children who were non-ambulant and profoundly disabled seem to have shown increased responsiveness and some developmental improvement.

Patterns of behaviour problems have shown some changes, with considerable improvement in some problems, but increase in others. There does not appear to have been any overall deterioration in behaviour of any of the children.

Contact with Paramedical Services

Reports from the physiotherapist and speech therapist indicate no decrease in contact or in activities prescribed and carried out, after placement in the mainstream schools. Progress reports are positive on all children.

PROBLEMS AND DIFFICULTIES

The interviews and records of the specialist support teacher and classroom assistants identify a number of problems that occurred in the course of the pilot study. The majority of these were resolved, but their identification provides useful information for future developments in integration.

1   The Commencement of the Pilot Study and Preparation

The records give the impression that the start of the project was too rushed and that more careful preparation could have avoided some problems and also provided better measures for evaluation. A period of observation and recording in Overdale School before placement of the children into the mainstream schools would have provided useful comparative data.

All classroom assistants started at the same time and worked in a class at Overdale with their individual children. This proved difficult to organise and it might have been easier if the start had been staggered.

Comment
This is a very good point. I cannot think why we found it necessary to place all the children in their mainstream schools at once, or employ all the classroom assistants at the same time. A staggered start would have been much better for all concerned.

All classroom assistants participated in a short EDY course at the beginning of the pilot study, but staff changes during the project meant that those starting afresh did not receive this. Three out of the eight classroom assistants interviewed did not feel adequately prepared.

Comment
Personally, as I have already made clear in Chapter 5, I feel that the EDY course, or any other course for that matter, was entirely unnecessary. Classroom assistants do not need a lot of information about behavioural techniques, teaching methods or general facts about children with learning difficulties. They need to form a sound relationship with the child they are going to support, and to learn from the child's parents, in practical terms, precisely what his special needs are. It would have been much better, therefore, if our classroom assistants had been based at the child's home for a period before entering into the mainstream school, rather than at Overdale School, where they began their acquaintance in an abnormal atmosphere of disability and with an emphasis on 'special'. It would also have been useful if we had allowed the classroom assistants to be placed in the mainstream classes without their children on regular occasions before the placement started, so that they could become familiar with the mainstream school and its routines, and get to know the class teacher and the other children in advance.

The amount of preparation in the mainstream schools varied. In two schools, the decision to take part in the pilot study was discussed with all staff by their head; thus their concerns could be expressed and recognised. However, the heads in the other three mainstream schools did not choose to do this. There was evidence of some negative attitudes among the mainstream staff, which proved problematic for the project in the early stages. Only 50 per cent of class teachers felt well prepared for the project. More information and preparation of mainstream staff by Overdale School and opportunities for expression of concerns might have been beneficial. If mainstream staff felt that they were faced with an unknown situation, this would have increased their fears and anxiety. The support of Overdale School would have been an important factor. In this respect, it was noticeable that at project meetings, heads of host schools were concerned that the children should remain on the register of Overdale School, thus providing access to the resources of the special school and a 'safety net'.

Comment

Whilst we advised the heads of mainstream schools to discuss their participation in our pilot study with the rest of their staff, we were not in a position to enforce this. I suspect that the reason heads of mainstream schools were so concerned that the child should remain on Overdale School's register was that they feared the Education Authority might take away the support of a full-time classroom assistant once the child had been established in their school. Many heads had learnt this from bitter experience in the past.

2   The Role and Responsibility of the Class Teacher

The involvement of the class teachers with the integrated children varied considerably and was dependent on the initiatives of individual teachers. Some teachers appeared to be very interested and willing to be involved in work with the child, others less so. Discussion of the expectation of the roles of the class teachers, both their own expectations and those of the project staff, before the commencement of the project, might have clarified the situation.

Comment

This was in fact done with both the headteacher and class teacher in every school. Remembering that class teachers were in a largely anxious state, I suppose that very little of what was said to them at this time actually sank in. It should be remembered, too, that the specialist teacher was there to support both the child and the staff throughout, so she was always on hand to clarify the situation.

3 The Role of the Classroom Assistants

Some classroom assistants commented on the fact that the job description they were given did not accurately reflect the tasks they carried out. The importance of their role on a day-to-day basis appeared to them to be underestimated. The low status and low pay accorded to them may have made them feel undervalued. In the interviews, some of them questioned their title, as they felt that some of the tasks they carried out were teaching tasks. It is not clear from the records that this was so and it seems likely that this problem resulted from misunderstanding of their roles. They certainly carried out tasks specified by the specialist teacher in the children's individual education programmes, under the supervision of the specialist teacher. However, whether this could be termed teaching is questionable. Their somewhat ambivalent situation, with a dual allegiance to the class teacher and the specialist teacher, resulted in a rather isolated role, although the specialist teacher arranged meetings between them to try to counteract this.

Comment

The job description that was prepared for classroom assistants was in fact turned down by the Education Authority who insisted on using their standard job description which they had designed for classroom assistants in special schools. It is therefore not surprising that they did not reflect accurately the tasks they were actually carrying out. The low pay and poor status were also commented upon in the report received from the North West Development Team, and I think this is a very valid point. As I mentioned before, perhaps the utilisation of the 'licensed teacher' concept would be one answer.

The presence of another adult in the classroom could be threatening for both the class teacher and the classroom assistant. It was seen by class teachers as a source of anxiety before the project. The fact that in only one case was there any significant problem in this area, and this due to a personality clash, attests to the competence and professionalism of both teachers and classroom assistants.

The amount of lifting required for one child and the uncertainties about how to deal with misbehaviour were also identified as problems for classroom assistants.

Comment

These are problems for staff whether they are based in a mainstream situation or in a special school. At least under the alternative special education system the teacher and classroom assistant have only one child to contend with, rather than a whole class of children who need to be regularly lifted or who exhibit some behavioural difficulty. They also have a specialist teacher on call who can be in situ to help, as well as a range of support disciplines that can be consulted wherever the child is placed.

---

4   Demands on the Specialist Teacher

The role of the specialist teacher has been crucial to the success of the pilot study. Her daily records indicate that considerable efforts went into her 'public relations' role, in trying to anticipate and avert any problems, treading carefully with 'host' schools and trying to avoid making any demands on them. This role was additional to planning and implementing, with the classroom assistants, the children's programmes of work, providing support for the classroom assistants and parents, assessment of progress and record-keeping. Her diary reveals that, on average, she was visiting five schools a day.

5   Staffing

Problems arose sometimes, in finding supply cover when classroom assistants were ill.

Comment

Again, these same problems exist when the child is educated in a special school. However, we were wrong to agree with mainstream schools that we would take on the responsibility for finding replacement staff in the event of absences. This was sometimes difficult for us to accomplish since we had to search out people in every area of Stockport who were police-checked and could stand in at the drop of a hat. This was unrealistic and would have been far better for the local school to make its own arrangements as it would normally do. For one thing, by tackling this task ourselves, we were preventing the inclusion of the classroom assistant as a fully integrated member of staff, which in turn reflected on the child.

6   Physical Resources

Lack of storage space for the equipment needed by two non-ambulant children and lack of privacy for changing them were slight problems. Overflow withdrawal space was also inadequate in some schools; sometimes corridors or cloakrooms had to be used. Open-plan schools, on the other hand, offered more space but any disruption caused by the child affected more people.

Comment

The problems of storage and privacy were only slight and were overcome fairly easily. The lack of space in some schools was simply a fact of life for them and their corridors and cloakrooms had always been used as teaching areas. It was quite normal for them to use these spaces for all children in the school, not just the child on our pilot study. Whilst floor space was at a premium, this had always existed and certainly was not caused by our adding just one more child to their roll. As far as open-plan schools were concerned, the disruption effect applied in respect of all children.

7 Visitors

The number of visitors involved in various studies of the project was particularly high. This placed extra stress on the specialist teacher in co-ordinating the visits, and on the 'host' schools.

Comments

The only other visitors involved in a study of the project, of whom I was aware, were The North West Development Team.

PERCEPTIONS OF SUCCESS

The overall conclusion from the data presented is that the pilot study was successful within its stated terms. The children do not seem to have suffered any disadvantage educationally, socially or medically from their placement in a mainstream school. Considerable social benefits have accrued from their interactions with other children and all of them have shown evidence of developmental progress. However, the degree to which this progress could be attributed to mainstream school placement, as such, is unclear. In addition, staff report benefits to the other children in the mainstream schools. The amount of integrated activity and one-to-one withdrawal varied between pupils. The profoundly handicapped children could not be left alone, but others could integrate into some group activities and in the playground without the classroom assistant. The constant presence of the classroom assistant with the child, if not handled carefully, could have acted as a 'gatekeeper', keeping other children from interacting with him or her. However, this does not seem to have been a problem. All reports confirm other children's positive response to, interest in and interaction with, the integrated pupils. Equally, the reported increases in the amount of work programmes completed by the children, and the evidence of their timetables, do not suggest that they suffered any decrease

in one-to-one teaching, compared with the situation at Overdale School; rather the reverse appears to have occurred.

An added bonus of the pilot study, noted by parents and the
specialist teacher, has been the increased parent-teacher contact.

To evaluate fully the degree of integration achieved by these
children, prolonged periods of observation would be necessary. However, some evaluation can be attempted from the
data presented. From this, it appears that, as the project
progressed, these children were accepted by and participated
in, their 'host' schools. Although the level of the children's
learning difficulties prevented full functional integration into
the whole of the mainstream curriculum, all the children were
socially integrated to some degree. The degree of participation
achieved, when viewed in relation to the children's own
functional capacities, appeared to be considerable for all children. This participation increased over time and may well
continue to do so.

RECOMMENDATIONS

These recommendations identify some areas where the evaluators feel improvements could be made in any future projects
of this type, based on the lessons learned from this study. The
overall success of the project suggests that extension to other
children could be feasible, but a number of areas of improvement should be considered.

1   The stated aim of not placing any demands on the
    'host' schools is unrealistic in any future broadening
    of the scope of this project. A longer and more
    structured preparatory phase would be necessary,
    where the responsibilities of the 'host' schools
    should be agreed.

Comment
We were certainly wrong to expend such great efforts in trying to avoid placing demands on the mainstream schools. It was counter-productive to the process of inclusion.

2 'Host' schools may in future be better prepared through:

a) Consultation between the 'host' school and the special school to agree the roles and expectations of the class teacher, specialist teacher and classroom assistant in relation to day-to-day responsibility for the child.

b) Preparation of and consultation with all staff in 'host' schools, providing opportunities for staff to gain information about the children with special needs, the role of the special school, the specialist teacher and classroom assistant; to express doubts and anxieties, negative and positive attitudes about the proposed placement. It is not suggested that a decision to accept a child should be unanimous, but that the acceptance of a staff's feelings is an important factor in prompting more positive attitudes.

Comment
The best preparation was when the supported child made short visits to the mainstream school prior to starting full-time. This enabled staff to see the child in a much less threatening light, rather than making themselves the victims of their own imaginations. Where admission to a school is concerned, I do not think that the staff of any school should have the right, or indeed the audacity, whether it be unanimous or not, to refuse any child a place in his local school, provided that any special needs he may have are adequately supported. Otherwise, we are simply condoning plain old-fashioned prejudice and discrimination.

c) Preparation of all classroom assistants for their role through spending time in the special school and through tutored time, such as EDY courses.

Comment
This I have tackled earlier (see pp. 78 and 154). To be based initially in a special school, with an induction into the use of behavioural techniques, is probably the least suitable preparation for classroom assistants that I can imagine, for the reasons that I have already given.

---

3   More accurate definition of the role of the classroom assistant should be reflected in the job description. The question of their responsibilities needs to be more carefully considered and defined. The low status and pay accorded to them do not seem to be entirely consistent with their perceived respon-sibilities in this study.

4   Arrangements for temporary cover for classroom assistants when off ill need to be clarified. In the case of a child who is totally dependent on the support of a classroom assistant, delays in provision of supply cover create problems.

5   Staff training is important for both classroom assi-stants and class teachers. In-service training related to children with severe learning difficulties would enable the class teachers to have greater confidence in being involved in work with children.

Comment
I believe that the most important training is for the class teacher to get to know the individual child well and to develop a clear insight into that particular child's special needs.

---

6 The demands on the specialist teacher should be carefully monitored. It may be that five 'host' schools are too many for one teacher, or that, with co-operation of the schools, visits to each could be timetabled to cut down on travelling.

Comment

Hazel, the specialist teacher, denies this and, in the light of her experience, thinks that nine children would be nearer the mark. This in fact is the number that has been supported by the specialist teacher over the past twelve months and it has presented no real problems. On the other hand, teaching these children in one class, under the traditional special school system, proved to be far more demanding and stressful.

7 It is important for the child's social contacts that placement in his or her local school should be given priority. Wherever possible, the local school should be approached and the importance of this, for the child's social contacts, should be discussed with the schools.

Comment

I entirely agree, placement within the local school is of paramount importance.

8 The data on contacts with paramedical services available from this pilot study showed that there was no significant decrease as a result of mainstream placement. However, any decision to widen such a scheme would be likely to have resource implications for the Health Authority, who would need to be consulted in the planning phase.

Comment
If the paramedical staff who are currently based in special schools were simply transferred to the local clinics and saw the supported children in just the same way as they already see other children who attend mainstream schools, then I fail to see what difficulties this would present.

---

9   In any future projects of this type, it should be recognised that the project commences well before the placement of the children. Careful record-keeping before and during the placement is necessary to ensure that the advantages or disadvantages to the children can be fully appreciated.

10   It must again be noted that, in the situation of this project, where parents and 'host' schools are generally committed to the integration of children with severe learning difficulties, successful outcome is unsurprising. However, it must not be assumed that the parents of all children with severe learning difficulties or heads of all primary schools would be equally committed. Nevertheless, the results of this pilot study may challenge some of the negative attitudes towards the integration of children with severe or profound learning difficulties, which were identified in the Educational Psychology Service survey (Tyler and Dodd, 1989) and have been found in other investigations.

Comment
At the beginning of the pilot study, parents thought that the ideas behind the concept of inclusive education certainly seemed to make sense. However, at this stage, nothing was proven and it was with a great deal of concern and courage that they allowed their children to take the first steps into a normal school life. Parents were by no means

committed to this until, with great relief, they witnessed the benefits. Heads of mainstream schools, likewise, were not committed to the notion of integration until after the pilot study was under way and they could see for themselves.

9 The Educational Psychology Service Survey

The Educational Psychology Service survey (Tyler and Dodd, 1989), referred to above, consisted of a questionnaire which was sent to all nursery, infant, junior and primary schools throughout Stockport, prior to the commencement of our pilot study. In all, 123 questionnaires were distributed and 86 were returned completed. This meant a return rate of 70 per cent. The data received were analysed by using a standard computer-based statistical package (SPSS-PC+). The results showed that two-thirds of these schools already accommodated children who had statements of special educational needs, although I suspect none of these had severe learning difficulties.

In the initial questions, headteachers were asked first to rate how they felt *in principle* about the inclusion of children with special needs into mainstream schools generally, selecting one of five answers: 'strongly disagree', 'disagree', 'agree/disagree', 'agree' and 'strongly agree'. They were then asked how they felt about the integration of children who have special educational needs into mainstream schools *in practice*. Figure 5 shows that a total of 82.5 per cent of headteachers either agreed or strongly agreed in principle, but this was reduced to 62.8 per cent agreeing and strongly agreeing in practice. Whilst there is no evidence in this particular study to show it, I believe that one of the reasons for this could well be that whilst headteachers are largely in agreement with inclusive education in principle, in practice they feel that they will

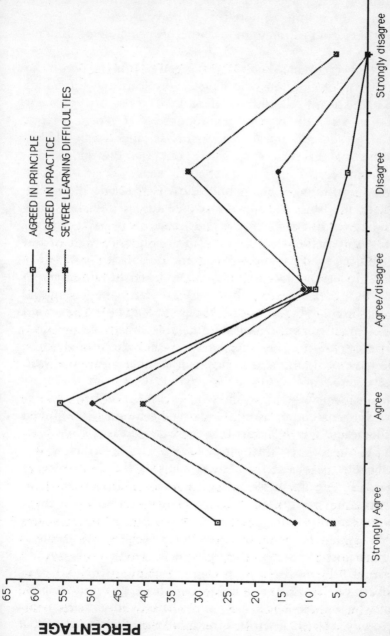

Figure 5. Percentages of teachers willing to consider children with special needs in their classes: in principle, in practice and if the children had severe learning difficulties.

be unlikely to receive adequate support with which to carry it out. It is interesting to note that nobody strongly disagreed with the notion of integration, either in principle or in practice.

Heads were then asked if they agreed in principle with the integration of children who have severe learning difficulties into mainstream schools, and the total of those in agreement and those strongly in agreement reduced to 46.5 per cent, but still a considerable number nevertheless, and we should remember that this survey was carried out *before* our pilot study. Unfortunately, to date no post-study survey seems to have been administered, which would allow us to see headteachers' attitudes in the light of experience. We do know that all heads who have participated in the pilot study now have positive attitudes in each of these aspects, in principle, in practice and for children who have severe learning difficulties.

The Tyler and Dodd survey then asked headteachers to rank, by order of ease, which of eight categories of special needs, shown in Figure 6, they thought could be incorporated into a mainstream school setting. The figure shows that, before our pilot study, headteachers thought that children who have profound and multiple disabilities and those who have severe learning difficulties would be by far the most difficult to include into their schools. As far as I am aware, however, no definition and standard description was supplied to the heads, which means that there could easily have been some confusion over the terminology used. Nevertheless, it is reasonable to assume from these statistics that headteachers regarded the bottom five categories shown as the easiest to integrate. I submit that this may well have been because these children are often already attending mainstream schools, and the heads therefore had some concrete knowledge to go on. It is quite possible that in the light of experience they would learn, like the heads participating in our pilot study, that all children can easily attend their local school, given the opportunity, whatever labels their special needs might be given. Certainly, in management terms, those children described as

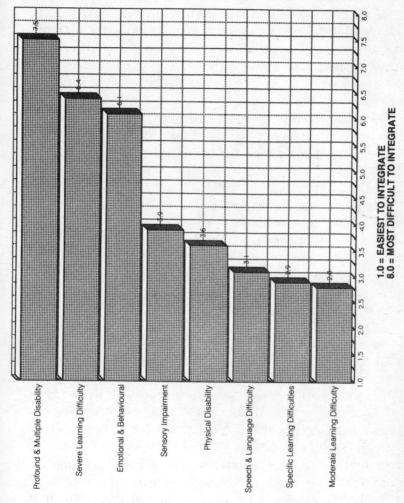

1.0 = EASIEST TO INTEGRATE
8.0 = MOST DIFFICULT TO INTEGRATE

Figure 6. Ranking special needs.

having profound and multiple disabilities are less likely to throw stones, climb walls and pick fights than their peers who are already in mainstream education.

Heads were then asked, by means of an open question, what factors might affect the successful integration of a child who has severe learning difficulties? The answers fell into five broad demarcations.

1   CHILD RELATED
    including nature of special needs
                    personality of the child
                    child's need for an individual programme

2   STAFF RELATED
    including training experience of mainstream teacher
                    the devising of programmes
                    the personality of the teacher
                    teacher's ability to cope under stress
                    attitude of the specific teacher
                    attitude of the staff
                    ethos of the school

3   PARENT RELATED
    including degree of support from child's parents
                    attitude of other parents
                    attitude of the community generally

4   ORGANISATIONAL
    including staffing level/staff–student ratio
                    need to give the child individual attention
                    availability of specialist advice/training/service
                    classroom assistants
                    class size
                    space
                    suitable buildings
                    equipment

materials
teaching aids
time
flexibility of class/school organisation
administrative resources
LEA support and funding

5   OTHER CHILDREN RELATED
  including ratio of mainstream to children with special
            needs
            recognition of other children's needs

If we read carefully through these answers, we can see that they manifest an underlying attitude which results in distinct discrimination against children who have a disability. It is an attitude which is rife within the adult population of our school system and within our society today, for these people are the products of a segregated education. If these same answers were applied to all children, not just to those who have special needs, as criteria for successful entrance into mainstream school, I suspect that there would be some very pertinent questions asked. Why, I wonder, should headteachers be concerned about, '**the personality of the teacher**' or have any doubts about '**the teacher's ability to cope under stress**?' Surely they do not believe that they are employing vast numbers of teachers who have adverse personalities and are unable to cope under stress. Similarly, it is a sad reflection that heads should consider '**the attitude of the specific teacher**' and '**the attitude of the staff**' significant factors which might prevent the inclusion of *any* child into their school. More than any of these, however, why should '**the ethos of the school**' be regarded as likely to militate against the inclusion of a child with disabilities? What sort of ethos could this be, and is it a desirable one for *any* school to have?

If these answers reflect the attitudes which generally exist among our school staff today, and I suspect that they do, then unless we begin the process of educating our educators,

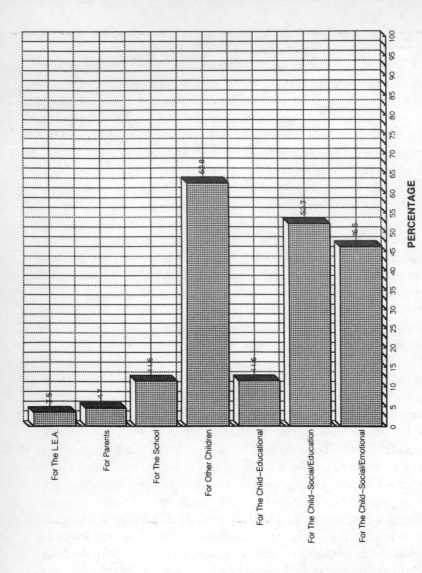

Figure 7. *Factors which heads thought might affect successful integration.*

minority groups within our society will continue to be ostracised from generation to generation.

I am sure that if children had been asked the same question as the headteachers, their lists of factors affecting integration would not have been anywhere near as long and complicated, if indeed there had been any lists at all. Still, it is interesting to see the nature of headteachers' insecurities in general, and the barriers they erect against disabled children and their families. Again, I do not suppose that these lists would be so comprehensive once headteachers had gained some experience of including such children into their schools. In percentage terms, Figure 7 shows that the great majority of headteachers' concerns are purely organisational, which is quite encouraging since it is probably the easiest barrier to overcome. It is reassuring to see, too, that the lowest percentage of doubt relates to the children themselves, whether they have a special need or not. Without benefit of experience, therefore, the aspect which headteachers believe would most greatly affect integration is its organisation, and their specific areas of concern are listed on p. 170. Looking at these, we can assure them that the **'need to give the child individual attention'** would in fact be met by the **'availability of specialist advice/training/service'**—in particular, by the provision of a full-time **'classroom assistant'** for each supported child, together with regular visits from a specialist teacher who, along with the child's parents and other professional disciplines, would supply the advice, training and service stipulated by the headteachers.

Since each local mainstream school would on average be expected to find a place for just one child with severe learning difficulties (people are often inclined to think that disabled children must be accommodated in large numbers, because our services portray them in this way, as always being together under one roof), then the worry about class size and the need for extra space is put into proper perspective. One single child, even if he or she is the biggest of children, does not take up that amount of space. No matter how you apply the mathematics, the additional pupil will still only turn a class of twenty-five children into a class of twenty-six.

'**Suitable buildings**' were another concern for headteachers. Whilst access can be a problem, this should be put in context. Not all children who have a severe learning disability use wheelchairs, but for those who do, a few inexpensive home-made ramps can usually enable them to gain access throughout most schools. As for '**equipment**', '**materials**', '**teaching aids**', '**time**' and '**administrative resources**', again, we should remember that these only need to be provided for one extra child, and in this context '**Local Education Authority support and funding**', can easily be made available, since it is already available in the form of special schools. If special schools no longer existed, then the current budget spent on them could be invested in supporting their pupils within mainstream schools.

Finally, the '**flexibility of class/school organisation**' that headteachers mention is entirely in their own hands and, in my humble opinion, the more organisational flexibility that exists in a school, the better will it be able to manipulate optimum learning opportunities for all its pupils.

Headteachers were next asked what advantages there might be, if any, in integrating children who have severe learning difficulties. Their answers were as follows:

FOR THE CHILD
a) *Social/emotional*
including experiencing acceptance
belonging to the community

b) *Social/educational*
including modelling/experience/identifying with 'normal' children
stimulation from normal children
diminishing behaviour problems

c) *Educational*
including reference to obtaining access to full 'normal' curriculum

FOR OTHER CHILDREN

d) including reference to the acceptance and understanding
            of others' needs
            development of caring attitudes/tolerance

FOR THE SCHOOL

e) including access to specialist help
            access to new materials/resources
            development of staff tolerance towards learn-
            ing difficulties and new teaching styles

PERCENTAGE

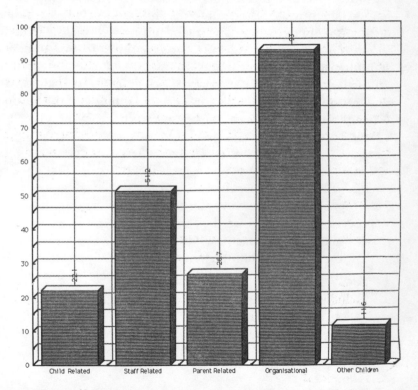

*Figure 8. Percentages of teachers indicating particular type of advant-
age for integrating children who have severe learning difficulties.*

FOR THE PARENTS
f) including acceptance by other parents
acceptance by the local school

FOR THE LOCAL EDUCATION AUTHORITY
g) including financial benefits

Figure 8 shows that, for the majority of headteachers, it was children, both those who have severe learning difficulties and those who have no special needs, who featured predominantly in what they believed to be the advantages of inclusive education. Advantages for the parents and the Local Education Authority were far less frequently cited. The most commonly named benefit was related not to the child with severe learning difficulties, but to the mainstream pupils, whom the heads thought would learn tolerance and acquire greater understanding of the needs of others.

When it came to the question of possible disadvantages of integration, Tyler and Dodd observed that many of the headteachers' answers were the antithesis of what they previously saw as advantages.

> Thus, for example, whilst it was felt by some that the child with severe learning difficulties would experience 'acceptance' into the community through the integration process, it was also feared by some that he might experience rejection. Similarly, whilst some expressed the view that the child would benefit from modelling of and identification with 'normal' children, others cautioned that the child might feel frustrated by an inability to match the other children in some desired way.

Again the heads' answers were grouped and listed under the following headings:

FOR THE CHILD

a) *Social/emotional*

including experience of rejection by other children
loss of caring
loss of child-centred environment of special school
unsettled features of the move from special education

b) *Social/educational*

including association of the mainstream school with failure
frustration of not being able to match other children
lack of opportunity to identify with other children who have special needs
over-stimulating environment

c) *Educational*

including lack of individual attention
lack of specialist instruction/trained staff
lack of equipment/space to meet needs
inability of child to make appropriate activity choices
unspecified reasons why the child wouldn't be able to make as much progress

d) *Medical*

including reduced access to paramedical services

FOR THE OTHER CHILDREN

e) including effects of disruptive behaviour of the child who has special needs
Too much teacher attention being given to child with special needs

FOR THE SCHOOL

f) including extra demands/pressure on staff

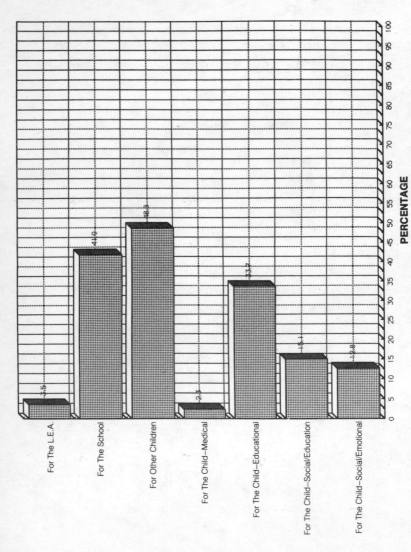

Figure 9. Percentages of teachers indicating each type of possible disadvantage from integration.

the tying up of resources
the lowering of general standards
parental opposition

FOR THE LOCAL EDUCATION AUTHORITY
g) including specialist resources being spread too thinly
    response time too slow

Figure 9 shows that headteachers thought that the disadvantages of integration would largely affect their own mainstream schools and their existing pupils. The mainstream children, they felt, would suffer from the effects of disruptive behaviour exhibited by children who had special needs, and that too much teacher attention would be diverted from them to the children with learning difficulties. This no doubt assumes that children with special needs would be imported into their classes in large numbers, rather than that they would be asked to absorb just one child into the whole school. It also makes unfounded assumptions about that one child, presupposing that his or her behaviour will automatically be disruptive and that this disruption will be greater than that created by the average child.

To begin with, unlike some pupils in mainstream schools, many children who have a severe learning difficulty are incapable of behaving disruptively, particularly those who have profound physical disabilities. Those who do would be managed by their classroom assistant, who in the last resort would be able to withdraw them from the classroom. More importantly, a co-ordinated common plan could be devised and carried out to enable the child to overcome this behaviour and to learn to conform. In this environment there would be large numbers of children to provide good models, as opposed to a special school situation which has fewer children but all presenting poor models of learning. The special school, despite its high ratio of staffing, is never staffed highly enough for them to be as consistent as they would wish to be. A certain amount of disruption, therefore, is often expected by special schools and tolerated, rather than conclusively dealt with.

The disadvantages that heads listed for their own schools included '**extra demands/pressure on staff**' which, in practice, would surely be pretty minimal in view of the fact that we are talking of merely one more child in the school, one who would have his own full-time classroom assistant and regular visits from a specialist teacher. '**The tying up of resources**' and '**the lowering of general standards**' would hardly result from adding one more individual to the school's roll, even if he were Al Capone jnr. As for '**parental opposition**' this has always been a worry for parents of the child with special needs, but in our experience it rarely ever exists.

In their discussion section Tyler and Dodd address six issues:

1   THE RESOURCE ISSUE
    'How are resources for children with special educational needs to be obtained and allocated?'

Comment
This is a question which could form the basis of another book, but in brief, resources that we seek are in fact already there, invested in great sums into a segregated special school system. These resources need to be taken from the special schools and, via local financial management arrangements, placed into mainstream education.

2   THE OWNERSHIP ISSUE
    'Who owns either the responsibility or the resources for meeting special educational needs?'

Comment
The receiving mainstream school, in the shape of its governing body, should own both the resources and the responsibility, if children with special educational needs are to be truly included, otherwise they will always continue to be 'the integrated child' or 'the statemented child', the one who is 'special', the one who stands out from the rest because of his need for 'different' things. Of course there will be those who say that budgets allocated for special needs will be misused by some heads

of mainstream schools and that the money will be used to buy resources for other needs in the school. However, the law requires that children who have their special needs recorded in the form of a statement must have these needs satisfactorily met. Governors of mainstream schools should therefore be expected to accept not only the additional funds, but also the legal obligations that go with them.

3   THE SUPPORT ISSUE
    'What services can support the mainstream school?'

Comment

In addition to each child having his own full-time classroom assistant and regular visits from a peripatetic specialist teacher, he and his school will also be entitled to all the support services to which he had access in the special school system—educational psychologists, paramedical staff, peripatetic teachers, educational advisers, school medical officers, social workers and so on. These could be made available much more readily if we stopped investing in buildings and started to invest in personnel.

4   THE FAILURE ISSUE
    'How do teachers in mainstream schools cope with the very slow educational progress that some children who have special educational needs are bound to make, relative to their peer group?'

Comment

In the same way as specialist teachers do, except that they will have the advantage of knowing that the specialist teacher and the child's full-time classroom assistant will be on hand daily, to assist both them and the child. In this way they may come to learn that we live in a world where everybody has a contribution to make, no matter who they are or what their academic ability may be.

5   THE PARENT ISSUE
    'How can schools make a positive response to the special needs of the parents as well as to those of their children?'

Comment

Like any service industry, schools should ask their service users (the parents) what they want, instead of giving them what they think they need. Some parents often say that they feel the need to meet other parents who have children with needs similar to those of their own child. Perhaps the school could provide its premises as a meeting place. Over a period of time, meetings like these could begin to include parents of children who do not have special needs, so that practical support and understanding could be encouraged to grow. One thing is sure: by accommodating their child in the local mainstream school, they would already have begun to meet these parents' greatest need, which is to be rid of the isolation they experience and to acquire a feeling of belonging.

6   THE POSITIVE DISCRIMINATION ISSUE
'Can staff accept that some children will receive more, in terms of resources, time, etc?'

Comment

These children will be receiving no more and no less than they already receive in a segregated system. The resources are not new, for they are already being allocated, but they will be used more effectively in mainstream schools. It is already recognised that because some children have extra needs they should have extra resources with which to meet those needs. After all, nobody begrudges a blind person a white stick or a guide dog.

Tyler and Dodd conclude their paper with an apt quotation. 'As one headteacher said,' they write:

'Integration boils down to, in the end, the attitude of teachers,' to quote Furnhar and Gibbs (1984). 'The major handicap of disabled people remains not so much their

specific disability, as the attitude towards them.'
Teachers need educating—it's the fear of the unknown;
they also need plenty of teaching assistance in the classroom.

10   Some End of Project Comments from Hazel, Our Specialist Teacher

Perhaps the one person who had an in-depth, yet overall view of our pilot study was Hazel Quinn. Hazel took on the role of our specialist support teacher and co-ordinated the day-to-day organisation of the project in all five participating schools. In April 1989, as part of the evaluation process, she expressed her thoughts on paper. These thoughts, with her permission, are reproduced below.

The pilot study has been running for a year now and I find that my attitude towards inclusive education has changed. I am now totally committed to the idea and have few doubts about it being the right way to educate children with special needs, severe or otherwise.

When I was initially asked to do the job, I was thrilled, but also slightly daunted. I knew I would enjoy the links between mainstream schools and special schools, but I also knew that attitudes in the 'outside world' towards children with disabilities can be hostile, sometimes not openly, and that to take on the role would at times mean putting myself in the line of fire of these hostilities. I also knew that to change attitudes towards disabilities, would be an extremely difficult task. However, it has been an exciting, varied and for the most part, enjoyable year for me.

In the beginning, when I heard the names of the children who were to take part in our pilot study, I was still more doubtful. I could clearly see those children whom I thought it would be reasonably easy to integrate, but the children who had profound and multiple disabilities, how were they going to cope with a mainstream school timetable in a mainstream school setting? I did worry and I did have doubts and reservations, but I didn't show any of these doubts or fears to our recipient mainstream schools. I sometimes confided them to Kenn, however, who was forever a cast-iron supporter, but never to anyone else, not even fellow teachers in Overdale School. I always showed a positive attitude. I feel that there are enough unjustified negative attitudes concerning integration, without my adding to them.

My job has covered a number of aspects and roles: public relations, support for classroom assistants and parents, my role as a teacher, administration and what I call 'spreading the gospel'. Initially, this was the battle against attitudes. I spent time reassuring headteachers and staff that the child from Overdale would not affect the smooth running of the school.

I tried to involve class teachers in decisions and asked them for advice so as to make the situation a two-way thing. I offered help whenever possible in small ways, like taking the class for the odd lesson and bringing in new pieces of equipment from time to time. I was careful to be in staff rooms at break times so that I could get to know all the staff and join in the general chit-chat. It is also very valuable to be aware of all the other issues, problems and events that are going on in a school. There might otherwise be a tendency to become blinkered and imagine that the schools had no other matters to deal with apart from our pilot study which after all, was a small part of their day. I found it useful to attend staff meetings at various stages of the project, so as to find out staff attitudes and any changes that might have taken place. These meetings have always proved very positive.

It is also most important to bear in mind other staff, especially caretakers, dinner ladies, cleaners and so on. It is better for them to be for you than against you, and it doesn't take much effort to spend some time talking to them, asking if they have encountered any problems and just explaining what it is we are endeavouring to achieve—and, of course, saying thank you.

The relationship with the classroom assistants can be a difficult one. They are the ones on the shop floor, so to speak, doing the actual 'integrating,' and I'm sure there must be times when they see me as just flitting off from one school to another, leaving them to tackle the nitty-gritty of everyday tasks. I have enjoyed working with the classroom assistants and must now throw in a few words of praise for their sensitivity and prudence in coping with a difficult task, whilst in receipt of a very poor rate of pay. As in any situation, relationships have been better with some classroom assistants than with others, it's a question of personalities. On the whole, though, I have enjoyed working with them all.

At first I thought it necessary to make all the decisions and plan all programmes of work myself, but as time has gone on, the decision-making and programme-planning has become a much more shared responsibility and, in my view, it is much more meaningful, if you are using something which you have been party to and helped to devise. I keep the classroom assistants supplied with necessary equipment and act as a link between headteachers, class teachers and other staff. We also have a great deal of telephone contact in the evenings.

This leads me on to the role of co-ordinator: arranging meetings, ensuring regular visits or attendance with support services like physiotherapists, teachers for children who have a hearing impairment, speech therapists and so on. I also set up outside activities like swimming and horse-riding. One of my biggest headaches has been to arrange supply cover when classroom assistants are absent through sickness. This has to be done in a way that causes all concerned as little inconvenience as possible.

My relationship with parents has been especially pleasing, as this new system allows me scope to fit in more home visits on a regular basis. I'm also available to any parents who want to speak to me on the telephone in the evenings. I feel that parents have been very brave subjects in this project and hopefully the results have rewarded this. I still like to keep my finger in the pie as a teacher and enjoy the opportunity of working with the children every week. I also like to become involved with the children in the mainstream school and this job has certainly provided plenty of opportunities for that. I now take the occasional PE lesson, do regular assemblies, music sessions and reading groups, with all the children in the school.

Whilst I still retain links with Overdale School, this has become more of an office for me, where I can consult with Kenn or with Chris, the deputy head, and where I can obtain resource materials. Initially I intended to have lunch at Overdale once a week, to keep in touch with the staff, but as time has gone on my relationships have grown stronger in the mainstream schools and less and less in Overdale.

On a final note, now that the pilot study has completed its twelve months of scrutiny, I feel that everything has become easier as relationships have established; instead of walking on eggshells, as I did initially, I find that I can make more demands on the recipient schools. Class teachers are much more involved, staff in general are much more willing to take on more responsibility, and integration is improving all the time. Changes of class teachers do not present as large a problem as they did initially. This has led me to question the value of strict programme-planning, and we intend to experiment in the near future by abandoning regular programmes in order to fit in with the mainstream lessons as much as possible. Strict programmes were needed at first, when everyone was finding their feet, but the amount of incidental learning that has taken place I'm sure outweighs that which has been achieved by traditional special school programmes of work. It has made me wonder at times whose needs we are actually meeting by producing a thick handwritten wad of detailed aims, objectives and programmed activities. This is the outcome of the general relaxation in attitudes within each school, which has meant that the children who have severe learning difficulties can be included in the mainstream system much more easily.

There have been moments during the last twelve months when I have felt frustrated and depressed—usually as a result of negative attitudes. This does take its toll and has sometimes made me feel quite low. However, I have always had firm support from Kenn and Chris and their convictions have given me the impetus to rise above these situations. In any case, these moments are soon forgotten when I see the whole system working so well within each of our five schools. I feel that their willingness to give our project a chance marks these schools out as places with true caring at the heart of them and with an interest in the education and development of all children who are to be our future citizens.

11 So Where Do We Go From Here?

Since the completion of our pilot study, other children from Overdale School (and some children who would normally have been destined for admission to Overdale School) have taken up supported places within their local mainstream schools and are progressing well. However, this has been accomplished on a rather piecemeal basis and, generally speaking, many parents are still having to struggle to gain a supported place for their child within the local school. Naturally enough, these families can and often do become very frustrated, since they recognise that the decision-making process adopted by most Local Authorities can grind exceedingly slowly and the action process even more slowly. Rumour has it that one education officer, somewhere in the Midlands, stamped frantically on a snail, because he said that it had been following him around all week! On the other hand, time being relative, it must seem to the families that the clock is ticking on at a rapid pace as they watch their child growing older by the day and wonder if he or she will ever be given the chance of a normal school life before it becomes too late.

Like any other Local Education Authority, Stockport has to juggle its finances, keeping all the balls in the air at the same time. It has to weigh in the balance, on the one hand, its commitment to provide quality education for everyone in the borough, together with its legislative obligations, and on the other, the finite resources it is given with which to accomplish this. It cannot therefore sustain for long a situation which is transient. Maintaining a school like Overdale, without offering any supported mainstream school placements to children who have severe learning difficulties, is just about financially bearable. The total closure of Overdale School will no doubt make it economically viable to offer supported mainstream places to *all* the children. Operating one system or the other is manageable, but to juggle with both, maintaining investments in a special school and granting full-time supported placements in local mainstream schools simultaneously, must be like standing on the centre of Tower Bridge with a foot on each side, watching it open. This is often the problem for District Health Authorities and Social Services Departments, who are enthusiastic about replacing institutions with innovative and exciting new services, but in the process face difficult monetary conundrums, in finding how to get from one system to the other without the need for bridging funds. I suppose that, where possible, the only practical solution is to close the old facility in its entirety at precisely the same time as opening the new one, but this is more easily said than done. Educationalists, however, do have a considerable advantage in that their services are largely not residential and are not therefore in essential use for twenty-four hours a day. Long holiday closures also mean that they have up to six weeks in which to complete any major changes that they may wish to make.

RESOURCED SCHOOLS

At the time of writing, Stockport Education Committee is again reappraising its delivery of special educational services. As far as Overdale School is concerned, having consulted widely, the Committee intends that it should shortly close. Somewhat disappointingly, what seems to be proposed to replace it at the moment is a system of 'resourced schools'. These are mainstream schools which are to be selected:

a) by their geographical location, so that chosen resourced schools will be evenly spread across the borough, mak-

ing them accessible to children who have severe learning
difficulties without long journeys;

b) by their positive attitude towards the concept of educational integration for children who have severe learning
difficulties;

c) by the degree of easy access and space available to
incorporate children who might spend much of their
time in a wheelchair.

It seems that each of these resourced schools will, initially at
least, be expected to cater for around six or seven children who
are currently attending Overdale School. The difference between such a resourced school and a mainstream school which
has a unit attached to it, in which to base children who have
special needs, is that a resourced school will absorb its intake of
children who have severe learning difficulties throughout the
main school itself, so that children are accommodated within
classrooms individually and age-appropriately. A resourced
school will also have added to its staffing an additional specialist teacher and two or three classroom assistants. These will be
ingested into the general economy of the selected mainstream
school's resources, and thereafter will be applied in practice, at
the discretion of the school itself.

In this way, I can see that the Education Authority is
attempting to create a wider spectrum of choice for parents
who have a child with severe learning difficulties. The Authority would, after all, be presenting these parents with the
option of a traditional form of segregated education, in the
shape of an existing special school (one which currently
educates children who have a physical disability and would, it
is proposed, change its character to include children with
severe learning difficulties). By the same token, the resourced
school would be made available to those parents who are
looking for a supported place in a mainstream school. This
may be viewed as a viable way in which the Education
Authority can be seen to be implementing its policy of inclusive education, by offering parents greater choice and at the

same time achieving this within the stringent financial restraints of its allocated budget.

Unfortunately, I fear that these resourced schools will only
go part of the way towards providing the complete alternative
special education system that many parents seek. To begin
with, within this reform, most children who have severe
learning difficulties still will not have the opportunity of
attending their *local* school, which the experience of our pilot
study and common sense tell us is so crucial to their inclusion
and to their development of a personal social network of
support. Also, the integration of six or seven children who
have severe learning difficulties, as opposed to just one child,
into a mainstream school is quite a different ball game. The
child's individual qualities and personality are inevitably lost
when he or she is relocated as part of a minority group. Under
these circumstances, their chances of being recognised as
Mike, Lizzie, Phillip, Lauren and Michael are low but their
chances of being identified as 'the handicapped children' are
remarkably high.

There should be concern, too, about the real future of
resourced schools of this kind. Just how they turn out in the
long run may not, I fear, be how we might envisage them.
While it is pleasing to see that planners seek to absorb children
who have severe learning difficulties throughout a school, one
wonders how this might be achieved in reality. After all, it
may well turn out that many of these children who live in the
same area are also about the same age. Under these circumstances, there may be a small group of children who not only
share the same age but who also have serious disabilities. Are
these to be accommodated together in the same classroom? I
think it much more likely that the headteacher will begin to
slip back into the special unit provision.

Similarly, what is to happen when new children who have
special needs seek to be admitted? Will the restrictions upon
Local Authority funding mean that the initial staffing ratio
will gradually become eroded, with the children being admitted one by one, without the staffing support being simultan-

eously increased? Where, too, will the staffing support be right from the very beginning for each child, if six or seven children are to be individually placed throughout the school, but only one specialist teacher and three classroom assistants are to be employed? This will mean that at any one time, a small number of children who have severe learning difficulties will always be unsupported.

Even with the best intentions of well-meaning education planning officers, sheer expediency, coupled with poor insight and lack of commitment, will undoubtedly gradually convert today's plans for resourced schools into tomorrow's special units. The inclusion of children who have special needs individually into their local schools is, I believe, the only sure way of even beginning to meet their needs effectively. The anxiety about its expense, which is often the primary concern of many budget holders although it is often well hidden or disguised, is I am convinced, over-calculated. Any anxiety there may be about its practicality is quite unfounded.

SECONDARY EDUCATION

When all the questions have been asked and answered; when all the 'what ifs . . .' and 'how abouts . . .' have been satisfied; when the last and most obscure hypothetical calamity that one could possibly imagine has been cited to test the argument which, after scrutiny, has still not been found wanting; when all the opposition to inclusive education has been totally exhausted with the logic and reason of the concept left intact, there still remains the one final resort of those who doubt: 'Ah but what will happen at secondary age, how will it all work then?'

To me, this always seems to suggest that, for some unaccountable reason, something quite mysterious happens inside our education system to people between the ages of eleven and sixteen, something which precludes participation by anyone who has special needs. Alas, I have never been able to discover just what this 'something' is. To some people, the notion of integration is quite feasible at nursery age, infant age and primary school age. It is also quite acceptable and even desirable within colleges of further education, adult leisure pursuits, housing and open employment—but secondary education? How, they ask, can students who have special needs ever go there?

It seems to me that applying the format of our pilot study is even easier within secondary schools than it is within primary education. For one thing, the breadth of curriculum in secondary schools is far wider than in special education. Arts alone take in a huge variety of painting, sculpture, dance, drama, pottery, music—the list is almost endless and far beyond the scope of the average special school for children who have severe learning difficulties. Then there are the sports, encompassing the full range of athletics, football, cricket, badminton, tennis, judo, trampolening—I could easily go on. And there are science laboratories and information technology, the like of which special schools are never likely to see. Then there are the budgetary resources that secondary schools enjoy. Their petty cash alone exceeds the capitation allowance that is made to most special schools.

We should remember, too, that inclusion is a two-way process and as such brings benefits to all students. Sometimes, in secondary schools, things like the teaching of woodworking skills, metalwork applications, electronics, and computer literacy can be more motivating if they are applied to the needs of other children. Making a towel rack is one thing, but asking students (if indeed they actually need to be asked) to design and make simple equipment that will visibly improve the quality of life for a friend in their class, can be quite another. The creation of opportunities like these would put caring into the curriculum of the mainstream schools and at the same time, economically provide what is often very expensive but essential equipment for others.

'Well, they reach their plateau, you know,' some say with great authority, as though children who have learning difficulties reach a certain age and then, unlike the rest of us, some mechanism shunts into place which prevents any further learning. I have been told as a 'known fact' that as children get older, the 'gap' widens. What this means, presumably, is that whilst most children will accumulate a larger repertoire of skills and concepts as they grow older, those who have severe learning difficulties will attain far less and at a slower rate. This seems more plausible to me than the 'plateau' theory, but the notion of the 'gap' seems to worry far more adults than ever it does children. As for it widening, this is not always so, since two of the children who participated in our pilot study are so profoundly disabled that it is difficult to imagine how the 'gap' could possibly get any wider than it already is. Despite this 'gap' being at its widest, the inclusion of these children into their local mainstream schools has been most successful.

If children who have learning difficulties do not proceed into mainstream secondary education, then the only alternative for them at present is attendance at a special school. Therefore, we should not be preoccupied with asking how they will cope at secondary age, but be concerned about the learning opportunities they will have within the confines of a special school, one which, as we have already established, is in comparison with a secondary school poorly resourced and poorly funded. Most secondary-aged special schools will emphasise the need for their students to attain as much independence as they can. In reality, the staffing ratios allocated to special schools are such that it makes individual tuition in actual situations infrequent at best. This means, in essence, that students have to develop and polish a range of self-help skills either within the confines of the building or as part of a class group in the real world. It is sad to see special school staff having to build large and magnificently constructed cardboard supermarkets within their classrooms, where plastic money changes hands for empty washing powder packets, simply because the real thing is inaccessible, even though it may be only a stone's throw away down the road. Even so, these will not be the students' local shops.

Under the pilot study system the secondary school becomes

the base from which learning can stem. The provision of a full-time classroom assistant and the regular support of a specialist teacher for each student means that we can provide the best of both worlds. Secondary schools are so organised that students are no longer taught by one teacher as they are in primary schools. Individual students follow a course of study through their chosen subjects and attend their own combination of personal learning modules. Those students who have severe learning difficulties are able to do exactly the same and at their own level of ability, once they have the supporting staff to assist them. A geography lesson about the rain forests of Venezuela may not be an appropriate learning situation, but learning their own local geography, how to get from home to school perhaps, or how to get around the school itself, may be very relevant. Whilst it is easy under the pilot study format for a student to learn how to use public transport to get from his house to the local swimming pool or cinema, on a daily basis if need be, this same learning situation, and others like it, are usually outside the reach of most special schools.

Whatever normality is, it is rarely to be found in special places. Those of us who are engaged in the planning and provision of human services must come to understand that, whilst some of the needs of some people may be regarded as special, the people themselves are not special at all. So often in our bid to enrich people's lives, we can and do, unwittingly, restrict severely the experience and opportunity of whole populations, who simply become the prisoners of our provision and the victims of our charity. Once they have been established, our conditioned attitudes can be passed down from parent to child and to their children's children, in family after family. Our stilted perceptions of those who are elderly, mentally ill, disabled or have a learning difficulty have now become so entrenched that any bid to alert us to our own shortcomings towards them, in our role as parents, relatives, professionals or neighbours, seems always to be viewed with suspicion and disdain. No matter how compassionate we may think we are, smug complacency can make us blind to the restraints, condescension and injustice that we inflict upon other people. Whether we are parents, relatives or professionals, it is useful for us to address the part we play in the lives of those near to us, who have special needs, and to ask ourselves, what is it precisely that we are contributing to, and is it what we would want for ourselves?

The education of young children is meant to equip them to live together in their adult lives, in a way that will build a peaceful, caring and prosperous future for each new generation that is to come. If we really believe in the pursuit of equal opportunity in our schools and in our society, if there is to be commitment to the underlying merits of a comprehensive education system, then everyone should belong.

Bibliography

DOLAN, Pat (1990). What Did You Do at School Today? in *Community Living*, Vol. 3, No. 3.

GATHERCOLE, Chris (1989). *Overdale: Integrating Children with Severe Learning Difficulties into Mainstream Schools*. Unpublished report for North West Mental Handicap Development Team.

JUPP, Kenn (1987). *Quality Education for All: The Integration of Children Who Have Severe Learning Difficulties into their Local Mainstream Schools*. Unpublished report for Metropolitan Borough of Stockport (Education Division).

JUPP, Kenn (1989). *Empowering Parents and Advocates in Stockport*. Pamphlet published by Overdale School, Stockport.

O'BRIEN, John (1981). *The Principle of Normalisation: A Foundation for Effective Services*. Adapted by Alan Tyne for the Campaign for Mentally Handicapped People (now Values Into Action) and CMHERA.

POOLE, Nick (1988). *The Overdale Project*. Unpublished paper written as part of MSc course.

QUINN, Hazel (1989). *The Overdale Pilot Study: Thoughts about the Last Twelve Months*. Unpublished report for Metropolitan Borough of Stockport (Education Services Division).

SLOPER, Tricia, and ELLIOT, Colin. *Evaluation of the Overdale Project for the Integration of Children with Severe Learning Difficulties into Mainstream Schools*. Unpublished report for Metropolitan Borough of Stockport (Education Division).

THOMAS, Sue (1989). *Open the Door and Let Us In*. Pamphlet published by Overdale School, Stockport.

TYLER, Steve, and DODD, Lynda (1989). *The Attitudes of*

Mainstream Schools Towards The Integration of Children with Special Educational Needs. Education Psychology Service Occasional Paper No. 1, Metropolitan Borough of Stockport.

TYNE, Alan (1980). *An Ordinary Life*. King's Fund, London.

WOLFENSBERGER, Wolf, with GLENN, Linda (1975). *Program Analysis of Service Systems (PASS): A Method for the Quantitative Evaluation of Human Services*. NIMR, Toronto.

Index